ANATOMY OF A SHIP

ANATOMY OF A SHIP
SCHARNHORST-CLASS BATTLESHIPS

DANIEL KNOWLES

FONTHILL

First published in Great Britain in 2026 by
Fonthill
An imprint of
Pen & Sword Books Ltd
Yorkshire – Philadelphia

ISBN 978-1-03615-696-1

A CIP catalogue record for this book
is available from the British Library.

Typeset in SabonLTStd 10/13 by
SJmagic DESIGN SERVICES, India.
Printed and bound in the UK by CPI Group (UK) Ltd, Croydon, CR0 4YY

MIX
Paper | Supporting responsible forestry
FSC® C013604

The Publisher's authorised representative in the EU for product
safety is Authorised Rep Compliance Ltd., Ground Floor,
71 Lower Baggot Street, Dublin D02 P593, Ireland.
www.arccompliance.com

For a complete list of Pen & Sword titles please contact
PEN & SWORD BOOKS LIMITED
George House, Units 12 & 13, Beevor Street, Off Pontefract Road,
Barnsley, South Yorkshire, S71 1HN, England
E-mail: enquiries@pen-and-sword.co.uk
Website: www.pen-and-sword.co.uk

or

PEN AND SWORD BOOKS
1950 Lawrence Rd, Havertown, PA 19083, USA
E-mail: uspen-and-sword@casematepublishers.com
Website: www.penandswordbooks.com

Contents

Introduction

The *Scharnhorst* and *Gneisenau* were both Scharnhorst-class battleships and were the second largest warships constructed to see service with the Kriegsmarine after the two Bismarck-class battleships—*Bismarck* and *Tirpitz*. Despite coming to stand in the shadow of Bismarck-class, the ships of the Scharnhorst-class played a more proactive role in the Second World War and were Germany's most successful battleships. The ships marked the beginning of German naval rearmament after the Treaty of Versailles.

The *Scharnhorst* and *Gneisenau* were the first ships to be officially classified by the Kriegsmarine as *Schlachtschiff* [battleships], whereas other German battleships had been classified as *Linienschiffe* [ships of the line] and *Panzerschiffe* [armoured ships].[1] While the Kriegsmarine classified the *Scharnhorst* and *Gneisenau* as battleships, during the course of the Second World War, the Royal Navy classified the two ships as battlecruisers, although after the war the ships were reclassified by the Royal Navy as battleships.[2] At the same time, it may be noted that while the Royal Navy classified the *Scharnhorst* and *Gneisenau* as battlecruisers, the 1940 edition of *Jane's Fighting Ships* classified both the Scharnhorst-class and the ships of the Bismarck-class as battleships.[3] In addition to this, the United States Navy classified the ships of the Scharnhorst-class as battleships. As a result, in English-language texts, the *Scharnhorst* and *Gneisenau* have been alternately referred to as 'battlecruisers' and 'battleships'.

While this work classes the *Scharnhorst* and *Gneisenau* as battleships of the Scharnhorst-class, it is worth noting, however, that some sources classify the two ships differently. *Scharnhorst* was the first of the two ships to be launched and is considered to be the lead ship of the class by some sources. Other sources, however, refer to the ships as being of the Gneisenau-class due to the fact that *Gneisenau* was the first of the two ships to be laid down and was the first to be commissioned into service.[4]

From the inception of their design, the ships of the Scharnhorst-class were subjected to a number of limitations. First and foremost were the provisions and restrictions that the Treaty of Versailles placed on Germany. Under the Treaty of Versailles, Germany was permitted to construct new vessels up to a displacement of 10,000t, with the treaty stating, 'Germany is forbidden to construct or acquire any warships other than those intended to replace the units in commission'.[5] The number of ships that Germany could possess was also restricted under the terms of the treaty with

Germany permitted to retain only six pre-dreadnought battleships, six light cruisers, twelve destroyers and twelve torpedo boats with a further two pre-dreadnought battleships, two cruisers, four destroyers and four torpedo boats in reserve.[6]

The navy allowed to Germany under the terms of the Treaty of Versailles amounted to a coastal force of questionable strength. As a result it was only natural that Germany's new naval leaders would wish to have the situation with regards to the strength of the Reichsmarine, as the post-First World War navy was called, improved at the earliest opportunity. During the early 1920s the first consideration was given towards replacing the pre-dreadnought battleships and the old cruisers with new vessels. The proposals for the replacement vessels were not easily put into practice; the Weimar Republic was politically unstable and faced continual changes of government.

Between the end of 1918 and 30 January 1933, Germany had twenty cabinets and twelve different chancellors, which allowed for little continuity. Financially, Germany was in a desperate state, with the reparations demanded by the victorious Allied powers serving to virtually ruin the economy, which lead to hyperinflation. It was

The cruiser *Emden*, laid down in December 1921 and commissioned in October 1925. The *Emden* was the first major vessel constructed for the German navy since the First World War.

not until the mid-1920s, when the economic situation began to stabilise, that the government began to look more kindly upon the requirements of the navy.

Despite the economic turmoil, some of the needs and requirements of the Reichsmarine were catered for. December 1921 saw the keel laid of the light cruiser *Emden*, which was launched in January 1925 and commissioned in October of that same year as the first major vessel of the navy since the First World War. The first new replacement vessel for a pre-dreadnought was 'Armoured Cruiser A', later named the *Deutschland*. The *Deutschland* was a *Panzerschiffe*, a vessel that would come to gain a more infamous name: the pocket battleship. Meanwhile, as Germany struggled economically and slowly turned its attentions towards the renewal of older vessels, the Allied powers began to look towards disarmament and arms limitations.

In 1922, Great Britain, the United States, Japan, France and Italy signed the Washington Naval Treaty, which resulted in the suspension of all capital ships under construction and the scrapping of all proposed capitals ships, whilst also placing a limit on the number and types of vessels that could be constructed. In this, it was proposed to scrap existing or planned capital ships to give a ratio of 5:5:3:1.75:1.75 to Britain, the United States, Japan, Italy and France. A ratio of 5:5:3 would also be applied to the tonnage of secondary vessels. With respect to capital ships, tonnage would be restricted to 500,000 for both Great Britain and the United States, 300,000t for Japan, and 175,000 each for Italy and France.

The Washington Naval Treaty achieved a remarkable reduction in existing and proposed battleships. While stipulating that no new battleships could be laid down until November 1931, the Washington Naval Treaty would run until the end of 1936. The 1920s stood out as a period in which the world's naval authorities and their governments appeared to be dedicated to ensure that the First World War really was the 'war to end all wars'.

Long before the Washington Naval Treaty expired, and before the 'battleship holiday' it brought about came to an end, a disarmament conference was held in Geneva, Switzerland in June 1927. The conference proved to be a spectacular failure. Italy and France did not attend, while Britain and the United States became deadlocked on the issue of heavy cruisers and British attempts to place further restrictions on battleships fell on deaf ears. Three years later, in 1930, a third naval conference was convened, this time in London. Under the agreed treaty, which was signed on 22 April 1930, and commonly referred to as the London Naval Treaty, the standard displacement of submarines was restricted to 2,000t, with each major power being allowed to keep three submarines up to 2,800t, and France one, while the number of heavy cruisers that could be maintained by each navy was limited.

On 9 December 1935 a second disarmament conference was convened in London, which culminated in the signing of the Second London Naval Treaty on 25 March 1936. Great Britain and the Dominions, the United States and France were all signatories of the treaty. Japan, which had signed the previous treaties, withdrew from the conference on 15 January, while Italy refused to sign the treaty, largely as a result of the controversy following its invasion of Abyssinia and the sanctions imposed by the League of Nations. The conference was intended to limit the growth in naval armaments until 1942; however, the absence of Japan prevented an agreement being reached on a ceiling for the number of warships that could be maintained by each nation. Like previous treaties, the Second London Naval Treaty limited the maximum size of the ships and the maximum calibre of guns they could be armed with. Under the provisions of the treaty, capital ships were restricted to a displacement of 35,000t and a gun calibre of 14in.

Meanwhile, in Germany, design work on the *Panzerschiffe* had begun in 1923, before a temporary halt in the design and development work was forced by the collapse of the economy in 1924. The then commander-in-chief of the Reichsmarine, Admiral Hans Zenker, pushed hard for the resumption of the design work, which resulted in three proposals being drafted in 1925. In total the Reichsmarine ended up with five potential designs for the new armoured ships. The designs varied from ships capable of 32kt and armed with eight 8in. guns to ships capable of 22kt and armed with 15in. guns. Eventually, the design that was selected by the Reichsmarine for the vessel that would become the *Deutschland*, which would have two sister ships, the *Admiral Graf Spee* and *Admiral Scheer*, was for a vessel armed with 11in. guns. The decision to arm the new vessels with this calibre of gun was consciously made in order to avoid provoking the Allied powers and to ease the pressures on design staff.[7]

In 1932 the Reichstag passed the *Schiffbauersatzplan* [Replacement Ship Construction Programme]. The *Schiffbauersatzplan* called for two separate phases of naval construction. The first phase, which was to last from 1930 to 1936, was to be followed by a second, which was to last from 1936 to 1943. This second phase of the plan was intended to break the limitations of the Treaty of Versailles in secret. The *Schiffbauersatzplan* came into effect in November 1932 under the overall control of the Reich defence minister, Kurt von Schleicher, in response to the doomed Geneva Disarmament Conference, from which Germany finally took her leave on 14 October 1933.

France, long considered Germany's principal potential enemy, reacted promptly to the appearance of the *Deutschland* and the construction of her two sister ships by placing orders for two larger battleships: the *Dunkerque* and *Strasbourg*. Displacing 26,000t and armed with eight 13in. guns in two quadruple turrets, the Dunkerque-class could attain a speed of 30kt. The *Dunkerque* was launched on 2 October 1935 and commissioned on 1 May 1937, while the *Strasbourg* was launched on 12 December 1936 and commissioned in April 1939. Undoubtedly other neutral powers noticed the construction of the Deutschland-class vessels but looked on with less alarm than the French did. The construction by France of the *Dunkerque* and *Strasbourg* was closely watched by the Germans and prompted a review of German naval planning.[8]

On 30 January 1933 President Hindenburg appointed Adolf Hitler as Chancellor of Germany. Although initially hesitant, Hitler, by March 1935, had declared Germany's sovereignty in defence matters and initiated a rearmament programme. The initiation of the rearmament programme led to contracts being approved for the two armoured ships 'D' and 'E', which were to be constructed in response to the Dunkerque-class. Displacing 20,000t, the ships were to be larger than the Deutschland-class, at 754ft (230m) long and 84ft (25.5m) wide. In the design of ships 'D' and 'E' emphasis had been laid on an improved protection scheme with an 8.6in. (220mm) armoured belt, a citadel of 2in. (50mm) and an upper deck with a thickness of 3.1in. (80mm).

The Panzerschiffe *Deutschland* in 1934. (*Lot-2275-67, National Museum of the US Navy*)

The main armament was set as 11in. guns. Some thought was given to equipping the new ships with eight guns in two quadruple turrets, similar to the arrangement on the Dunkerque-class, as opposed to six guns in two turrets as on the Deutschland-class. However, this would have required a completely new design.

The traditional 5.9in. (15cm) gun was retained for the secondary armament alongside 3.9in., 1.5in. and 0.7in. (10cm, 3.7cm and 2cm) anti-aircraft guns. The installation of torpedo tubes was also envisaged. Lengthy discussions were subsequently held concerning the desirability of matching the 13in. main armament of the French ships. Consideration was also given to 14in. and 15in. guns, but as had been the case with the quadruple turret idea, a completely new design would have been required in order to mount them. Furthermore, Hitler would not have given this proposal approval, since for some time he had been making overtures to Great Britain. It is reasonably certain that Hitler was anxious at the time for reconciliation with the world's leading naval power and that by opting for a calibre of gun larger than 11in., this would have been likely to jeopardise the negotiations which led to the Anglo-German Naval Agreement.

During a speech delivered in Berlin on 21 May 1935, Hitler formally offered to discuss a treaty limiting Germany to a navy 35 per cent the size of the Royal Navy. The following day the British Cabinet voted to formally take Hitler up on his offer. Talks between the British and German delegations began on 4 June 1935, during which it was agreed that Germany could construct a navy on the ratio of 35:100. The German delegation conceded that the 35:100 ratio would be expressed in ship tonnage, with Germany building her tonnage up to whatever the British tonnage was across various warship categories. On 18 June 1935 the Anglo-German Naval Agreement was signed in London by the German foreign minister, Joachim von Ribbentrop, and the British Foreign Secretary, Sir Samuel Hoare.[9]

Five months after they were ordered, the keels of the two D-class vessels were scrapped on the stocks in order to make way for two new vessels which would become the *Scharnhorst* and *Gneisenau*. The provisional names of the two D-class vessels, *Ersatz Elsass* and *Ersatz Hessen*, were reallocated to new ships, the contracts for which were awarded to the Kriegsmarinewerft Wilhelmshaven and Deutsche Werke in Kiel. In cancelling the D-class, it was decided that the new vessels should be enlarged, so as to counter the Dunkerque-class. Work was, however, delayed for fourteen months in order to allow Hitler to preliminarily secure the Anglo-German Naval Agreement.[10] In addition to this, work was partly delayed due to numerous design changes implemented after the ships were ordered.[11]

From a political perspective, the construction of battleships 'D' and 'E' was a clear breach of the Treaty of Versailles. So too was the declaration of military sovereignty made on 16 March 1935. The tonnage of the armoured cruisers 'B' and 'C', which would become the pocket battleships *Admiral Scheer* and *Admiral Graf Spee*, also amounted to an infringement of the Treaty of Versailles. However, the culpability for this infringement lay with the pre-Hitler German governments and Reichstag. The building of battleships 'D' and 'E' was sanctioned retroactively by the Anglo-German Naval Agreement.

The building contract for Panzerschiffe 'E' was placed at the Deutsche Werke, Kiel on 25 January 1934. At the time that the contract was placed for the construction of the ship, final approval for the design had yet to be received. Nevertheless, on 14 February the keel was laid. Construction work on the hull was suspended on 5 July, and the work subsequently scrapped as the original plans were modified. Under the designation Construction Number K235 a new keel was laid afresh on Slipway One of the Deutsche Werke on 6 May 1935. On 8 December 1935, the hull of the ship was christened *Gneisenau* and launched. Subsequently, *Gneisenau* underwent a period of fitting-out work before being commissioned into the Kriegsmarine under the command of *Kapitän zur See* Erich Förste on 21 May 1938.

Meanwhile, the contract for the construction of Panzerschiffe 'D' was placed with the Marinewerft, Wilhelmshaven on 25 January 1934. As with the *Gneisenau*, at the time that the contract was placed, final approval for the design of the ship had yet to be received. The keel of the ship was also laid on 14 February 1934, with work proceeding on the hull until 5 July, when construction was halted and the decision taken to scrap the work already completed, as the original plans had been modified in order to accommodate the new ship specifications. From 1935 the Marinewerft was renamed the Kriegsmarine Werft, and it was here that the keel was laid afresh on 15 June 1935, under the designation Construction Number 125. The hull spent almost sixteen months on the slipway before being launched on 3 October 1936 and christened *Scharnhorst*. In attendance at the launching ceremony were Hitler and the minister for war, *Generalfeldmarschall* Werner von Blomberg. The *Scharnhorst* would spend the next twenty-seven months undergoing fitting-out work which saw the installation of her deck, armament and upper works.[12] With the fitting-out work completed, on 7 January 1939 *Scharnhorst* was commissioned into the Kriegsmarine under the command of *Kapitän zur See* Otto Ciliax.

War returned to Europe in September 1939. Once war had been declared on Germany, the Royal Navy sought to enact and enforce a blockade of Germany as in the First World War. Under the designation Northern Patrol, British forces sought to prevent trade to and from Germany by checking merchant ships and their cargoes. In addition to this, the Northern Patrol was to stop German warships and raiders from leaving the North Sea and entering into the Atlantic and vice versa, protect the Shetland Islands from invasion, and gather intelligence from intercepted neutral ships. The Northern Patrol had previously existed between 1904 and 1917. Three days after Britain declared war on Germany in 1939 the force was reactivated. The reactivated Northern Patrol was given a more extensive area of operations than in the First World War, now including the areas north of Scotland and Ireland, between the north of Scotland and Norway, and around the Shetlands, the Faeroe Islands, Iceland and the Denmark Strait. As in the First World War, older cruisers from the reserve fleet made up the original units of the Northern Patrol; however, these were soon supplanted and replaced by armed merchant cruisers.

It was against this backdrop that, flying the flag of Admiral Wilhelm Marschall, at 14.00 on 21 November *Gneisenau* departed Wilhelmshaven in the company of *Scharnhorst* with the intention of breaking through to the area between Iceland and the Faroe Islands, before moving into the waters covered by the Northern Patrol. At that point a feint would then be made into the North Atlantic in an effort to draw off the ships of the Northern Patrol and disrupt British shipping.

On 23 November, the two ships sighted smoke on the horizon belonging to the armed merchant cruiser HMS *Rawalpindi*. A former liner on the British route to India, which had been requisitioned by the Admiralty at the outbreak of war, she was no match for either *Scharnhorst* or *Gneisenau*. Signals were made for the *Rawalpindi* to be abandoned, however, her commanding officer, Captain Edward Kennedy, elected to engage. The engagement lasted approximately fifteen minutes before a shell from *Scharnhorst* found the forward magazine of the *Rawalpindi*, which detonated and tore the ship apart. From the *Rawalpindi* 238 men would lose their lives, with thirty-seven being pulled from the icy waters by *Scharnhorst* and a further eleven later being rescued by another armed merchant cruiser.[13] The two battleships managed to evade subsequent British patrols and returned to Germany.

In April 1940, *Gneisenau* and *Scharnhorst* provided cover to the German invasion of Denmark and Norway and on 9 April conducted a brief running engagement with the British battlecruiser *Renown*. On 4 June, *Gneisenau*, flying Marschall's flag, and *Scharnhorst* were once more at sea as part of an operation to resupply German forces around Narvik. On 7 June, Marschall decided to take *Gneisenau* and *Scharnhorst* and to move to a position to operate against British convoys evacuating Norway. During the afternoon of the following day, the two German ships stumbled upon the aircraft carrier *Glorious* and her escorting destroyers *Ardent* and *Acasta*. At the time, *Glorious* was at a low state of readiness.

Gneisenau opened fire against *Ardent* at 16.27. The engagement lasted until 18.25. At 18.10, following a sustained bombardment, *Glorious* sank, losing all but forty-three of her crew.[14] *Acasta* and *Ardent* too succumbed after a violent bombardment and sank at 18.20 and 18.25 respectively. The engagement was not, however, one-sided. *Ardent* succeeded in conducting five torpedo attacks against *Scharnhorst*. *Acasta* also launched a torpedo attack, with one torpedo striking *Scharnhorst* in the vicinity of turret 'Caesar', which caused extensive flooding and resulted in the deaths of two officers and forty-six ratings.[15]

Scharnhorst subsequently made for Trondheim, where temporary repairs were enacted before returning to Germany. Whilst undergoing temporary repairs, she was subjected to an attack whilst at anchor by Blackburn Skuas of the Fleet Air Arm. *Gneisenau* remained at sea conducting operations and was damaged in a torpedo attack conducted by the submarine *Clyde*. She too underwent temporary repairs at Trondheim before returning to Germany.

The two ships remained in home waters for the remainder of the year before, in early 1941, embarking on one of the most successful commerce raiding operations of the Second World War by capital ships, Operation Berlin. Under the command of Admiral Günther Lütjens, *Gneisenau* (once more serving as flagship) and *Scharnhorst* departed Germany and proceeded into the North Atlantic by way of the Denmark Strait. On 8 February the convoy HX-106 was sighted but not engaged owing to the presence of the battleship *Ramillies*. On 22 February the two ships stumbled upon a group of five unescorted merchant ships, which were then sunk. A further vessel was sunk on 9 March before thirteen vessels were sunk and three captured as prizes between 15–16 March. On 21 March, the two ships arrived at Brest, on the French Atlantic coast.

Operation Berlin lasted sixty days and saw the ships cover 17,800mi (28,646km) a record for German capital ships. During the course of the operation twenty-two merchant vessels totalling 113,690 gross registered tons were sunk or captured. Two days following the arrival of the battleships, the two tankers which supported the latter stages of the operation, the *Uckermark* and *Ermland*, docked at La Pallice, an outer port of La Rochelle which had been constructed to accommodate large oceangoing passenger liners. Following arriving at Brest, aboard *Gneisenau* Lütjens and his staff set about packing their bags in preparation for a return to Germany where they had orders to join the battleship *Bismarck* for a new operation.

The two ships would remain at Brest throughout the remainder of the year and into 1942. In June 1941 they were joined by the heavy cruiser *Prinz Eugen*. Whilst at Brest, the ships were subjected to numerous attacks by RAF Bomber Command and Coastal Command. On 13 November 1941 Hitler met senior officers of the Wehrmacht, Kriegsmarine and Luftwaffe at the Wolfs Lair, his headquarters in East Prussia. During the conference, Hitler declared that 'every ship which is not stationed in Norway is in the wrong place'.[16] Plans were subsequently drafted to return the three ships at Brest to Germany.

On 11 February 1942, Operation Cerberus began. It was one of the most audacious operations of the war which saw *Scharnhorst*, *Gneisenau* and *Prinz Eugen*, under the command of Vizeadmiral Otto Ciliax who flew his flag aboard *Scharnhorst*, depart Brest during the evening of 11 February and sail directly through the English Channel to Germany. Dawn on 12 February saw the ships in the Straits of Dover, the narrowest part of the Channel. It was only then that the British responded. The British response was confused. Subjected to ineffective fire from British shore batteries around Dover, the ships were attacked during the course of the day by aircraft of the Fleet Air Arm, Bomber Command and by British destroyers. The attacks were ineffective. *Prinz Eugen* made it safely to Brunsbüttel on the Elbe, dropping anchor on the morning of 13 February, where she was joined by *Gneisenau*, while *Scharnhorst* proceeded to Wilhelmshaven. Both battleships did not make it to Germany unscathed for *Scharnhorst* struck two mines and *Gneisenau* one whilst sailing along the Dutch coast.

Having reached Germany, both ships were taken in hand for repairs to be conducted. On the night of 26–27 February 1942, the RAF launched a heavy air raid against Kiel, where *Gneisenau* was drydocked.[17] A single bomb struck the forecastle and penetrated the armoured deck before exploding.[18] Hot fragments from the bomb ignited the propellant charges in the forward turret, causing an enormous explosion which served to throw turret 'Anton' off its mount and burned out the entire bow section.[19] The extensive damage that was sustained by the *Gneisenau* from the explosion of the forward turret convinced the *Oberkommando der Marine* (Upper Command of the Navy) to rebuild the *Gneisenau* in order to mount six 15in. guns, as originally planned. On 4 April, escorted by the training ship *Schlesien* and the icebreaker *Castor*, the *Gneisenau* sailed to Gotenhafen. By early 1943 the ship had been sufficiently repaired to enable the process of up-gunning the ship from 11in. to 15in. guns to begin. Events conspired against the *Gneisenau*, however, for Hitler, angered at the performance of the *Admiral Hipper* and *Lützow* during the Battle of the Barents Sea, decided to scrap the entire surface fleet of the Kriegsmarine. While *Großadmiral* Karl Dönitz managed to save a significant number of vessels from being decommissioned and sent to the breakers yard, the cessation of work on the *Gneisenau* was ordered.[20]

In the wake of this decision, *Gneisenau* was disarmed and used for spare parts. Reusable parts of the ship were scavenged and used to repair and maintain the remaining elements of the Kriegsmarine's surface assets. The main and secondary armament of the ship were removed in order to be used as gun batteries.[21]

The hull of the *Gneisenau* remained in Gotenhafen until the end of the war. As the Red Army advanced on the city, the remains of the ship were taken out to the entrance of the harbour and scuttled as a blockship on 27 March 1945. The following day the city fell to Soviet forces and was assigned to the Gdańsk Voivodeship, who renamed the city Gdynia. In 1947 the Polish government ordered that the remains of the *Gneisenau* be removed from the harbour entrance, prompting salvage operations to begin.[22] The hull was sealed and re-floated on 12 September 1951 before being towed away for scrapping.[23] It is believed that some of the steel from the *Gneisenau* was subsequently used in the construction of Polish merchant vessels.[24] When she was re-floated on 12 September 1951, the *Gneisenau* was the largest ship to ever be raised.

On 8 March 1943, following repairs, refitting and a period in the Baltic, *Scharnhorst* was transferred to Norway. Proceeding to Altafjord, where she joined the *Tirpitz*, the ship acted as part of a fleet in being. In September, she weighed anchor and embarked on an operation with the *Tirpitz* to bombard the Allied weather station on the island of Spitzbergen. She was also a target of British midget submarines, known as X-craft, during Operation Source. Absent from her anchorage conducting exercises, she succeeded in avoiding damage, while *Tirpitz* was put out of action, rendering her the sole German capital ship in northern waters.

On Christmas Day 1943 *Scharnhorst* put to sea for the final time, to intercept the convoy JW-55B, bound for Murmansk. The following day, Boxing Day 1943, she was sighted at around 09.00 and engaged by the British cruisers *Belfast*, *Norfolk* and *Sheffield*. Struck twice by the British cruisers, *Scharnhorst* used her superior speed to break off the engagement. The British cruisers regained contact with *Scharnhorst* around noon. Once more the superior speed of the *Scharnhorst* allowed the battleship to break off the engagement, although she continued to be pursued by the British cruisers. At 16.17 *Scharnhorst* was picked up on radar by the British battleship *Duke of York*. Shortly before 17.00 *Duke of York* opened fire with her 14in. guns. A running duel subsequently began in which *Scharnhorst* exchanged fire with *Duke of York* and the cruiser *Jamaica* whilst also being subjected to torpedo attacks by British destroyers. Hit in the boiler room, which reduced her speed, *Scharnhorst* began to be pounded into submission as further torpedoes struck the ship. At approximately 19.45, the *Scharnhorst* capsized and sank, leaving behind a mere thirty-six survivors.

The construction of the *Scharnhorst* and *Gneisenau* as part of the German rearmament programme was more politically than militarily motivated. Their construction was completed against the backdrop of momentous political change in Germany and Europe, which heavily influenced their design. From the inception of the design, planning and construction, the Scharnhorst-class were subject to several limitations, first and foremost being the provisions and restrictions of the Treaty of Versailles. The ships represented a compromise on political grounds. Their design was ultimately not thought through from a military point of view.

Despite this, *Scharnhorst* and *Gneisenau* met with great success, especially when compared with the *Bismarck* and *Tirpitz* and other German surface vessels. German surface vessels. They successfully sank the armed merchant cruiser *Rawalpindi* and sank the destroyers HMS *Ardent* and *Acasta* along with the aircraft carrier *Glorious*. In addition to this they sank twenty-two merchant vessels totalling 113,690 gross registered tons. Furthermore, they helped to humiliate the Royal Navy, RAF and Britain in general with their daring dash up the English Channel. Whilst being the most successful German capital ships of the war, when taken as part of the German war machine as a whole, the accomplishments of the *Scharnhorst* and *Gneisenau* were none too impressive.

By the beginning of March 1942 U-boats had sunk a total of 5.5 million tons of Allied merchant shipping while aircraft had sunk almost 2 million tons. Surface raiders, by contrast, had succeeded only in sinking 363,146t. In addition to this, U-boats and aircraft had shown themselves to pose a bigger threat to the Royal Navy's capital ships than were the battleships of the Kriegsmarine. Only two capital ships of the Royal Navy, the aircraft carrier HMS *Glorious* and the battlecruiser HMS *Hood*, were sunk by capital ships of the Kriegsmarine. The six other Royal Navy capital ships lost up to the beginning of March 1942, which numbered three battleships, one battlecruiser and two aircraft carriers, were all sunk by aircraft or U-boats.[25]

Scharnhorst and *Gneisenau* could without doubt have been better used by the Kriegsmarine, perhaps in coordination with the *Bismarck*, had she not been sent on her ill-fated voyage of May 1941. Ultimately, the surface fleet of the Kriegsmarine lost out to the U-boat fleet. To compound matters, there was little experience at the top levels of German naval high command on how best to use the ships of the Kriegsmarine. Ships like the *Scharnhorst* and *Gneisenau* took up vast quantities of steel, took many man hours to construct and cost millions of Reichsmark, not to mention that 1,600 to 2,000 officers and sailors were required to crew the vessels and a vast quantity of fuel oil was required to fill the bunkers of each of the ships.

This does not, however, detract from the resources that the Royal Navy and RAF had to divert to attacks on the ships in attempts to destroy them. While *Gneisenau* met with what may be deemed an inglorious end, *Scharnhorst* holds a special place in history for fighting the last battleship engagement between British and German naval forces, which would also prove to be the penultimate battleship engagement in history.

1

General Characteristics

At the waterline the ships of the Scharnhorst-class were both 741ft, 6in. (226m) long. Despite possessing the same length at the waterline, the two ships differed in their respective overall lengths. *Scharnhorst* had an overall length of 771ft, 8in. (234.9m) while *Gneisenau* was slightly shorter, having an overall length of 753ft, 11in. (229.8m). Both ships had a beam of 98ft, 5in. (30m) and were designed to displace 35,540t, which would have given the ships a draught of 29ft, 10in. (9.1m). With a standard displacement of 32,600t, the draught of the Scharnhorst-class was reduced to 27ft, 3in. (8.3m), while at full load the ships displaced 38,100t, whereupon their draught increased to 32ft, 6in. (9.9m).[1]

Within the Kriegsmarine the ships of the Scharnhorst-class were considered poor sea boats; they were bow heavy when at full load and were very 'wet' as high as the bridge, with the forward battery turret, known as turret 'Anton', suffering from flooding in heavy seas. The problem of being wet ships was something which was mitigated to an extent by the replacement of the stem. As originally completed, both *Scharnhorst* and *Gneisenau* had a straight stem. However, in an effort to improve their seakeeping, both vessels had their original straight stems replaced with an 'Atlantic bow'. The Atlantic bow was, in effect, a flared bow, the design of which increased its lift ability. The Atlantic bow allowed the ships to gain more freeboard and sheer. The fitting of the Atlantic bow also saw the forecastle extended beyond the forward perpendicular (bow waterline point), which increased the sheer further and helped to direct water away from the forecastle. In the case of the *Gneisenau*, the ship was taken in hand in October 1938 for a refit, during which her straight stem was replaced by the Atlantic bow.[2] *Scharnhorst*, meanwhile, was taken in hand in a 40,000 ton floating dry dock at the Kriegsmarinewerft in July 1939 to have her straight stem replaced with an Atlantic bow.[3]

Despite being fitted with an Atlantic bow, it is worth noting that turret 'Anton' on both ships would remain restricted when operating in heavy seas.[4]

The stern of the ships of the Scharnhorst-class was also frequently wet and the ships were somewhat sluggish when entering a turn. In shallow water, the handling and response to the helm of both ships was considered to be so poor that they almost always required the assistance of tug boats. With hard rudder the ships lost over

50 per cent speed and heeled over more than 10°. During the course of their sea trials, in some instances, the ships heeled over as much as 13° when hard rudder was applied at speed.[5]

Both the *Scharnhorst* and *Gneisenau* had a crew of between fifty-six and sixty officers and between 1,613 and 1,780 enlisted men. The crews of the respective ships were augmented by a further ten officers and sixty-one men when they took on the role of squadron flagships.

	Scharnhorst	***Gneisenau***
Building costs	143.5m Reichsmark	146.2m Reichsmark
Measurement (net registered tons)	19,401	19,401
Displacement (full load)	38,100t	38,100t
Length (overall)	771ft, 8in. (234.9m)	753ft, 11in. (229.8m)
Length (waterline)	741ft, 6in. (226m)	741ft, 6in. (226m)
Maximum draught	32ft, 6in. (9.9m)	32ft, 6in. (9.9m)
Speed (knots)	31.5	31.3
Range (at 19kt)	8,200mi (13,100km)	7,100mi (11,500km)
Bunker capacity (tons)	6,200	6,200
Ship's company	60 officers, 1,908 men (1943)	56 officers, 1,613 men (1939)

The crests of the *Scharnhorst* and *Gneisenau*. (*Author's Collection*)

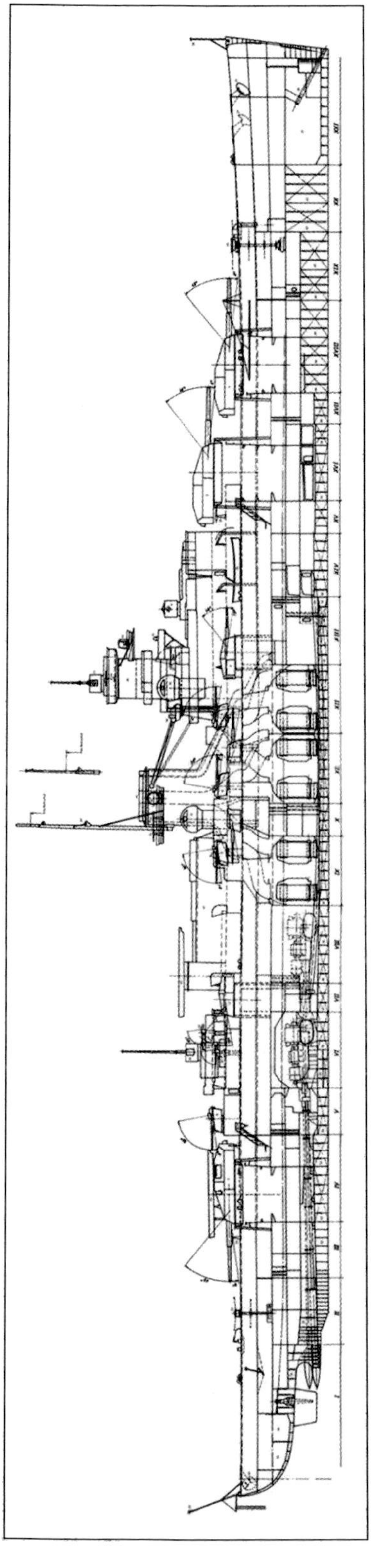

Longitudinal plans of the Scharnhorst-class.

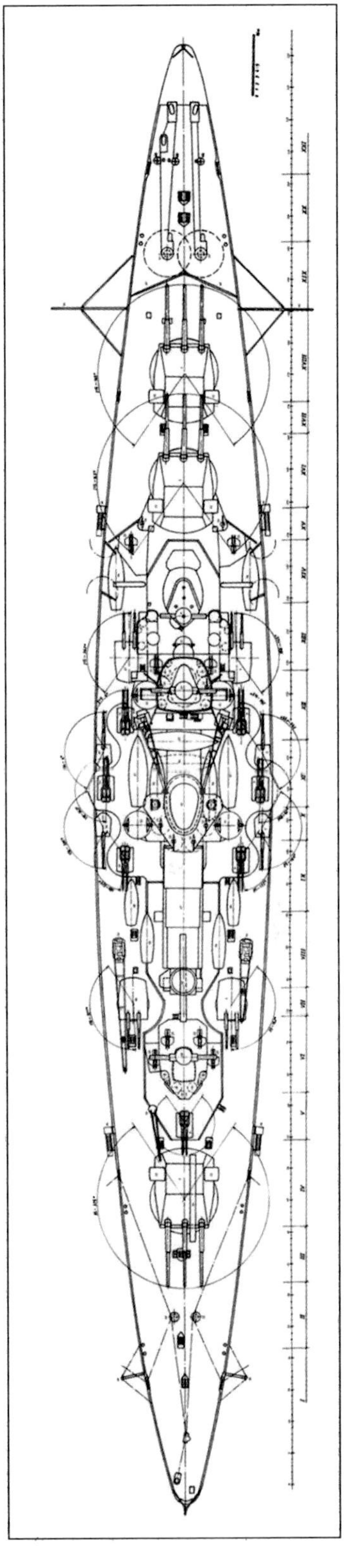

Upper deck plans of the Scharnhorst-class.

2

Armament

The primary armament of the Scharnhorst-class was the 11in. SK C/34 quick-firing gun sited in three triple turrets. They were arranged two forward, which were superfiring, and one aft known from bow to stern as 'Anton', 'Bruno' and 'Caesar'.[1] Up to the end of the First World War, in Germany, naval guns were known as *Schiffskanone*, which was abbreviated to SK and followed by the nominal overall length in calibres. During the interwar period the length was replaced in new gun designs by the nominal date, expressed by the last two figures of the year.[2] For instance, in the case of the SK C/34, the '34' refers to 1934. Mountings were known as *Drehscheibenlafette* abbreviated to DrhL, which meant 'turntable mounting'.[3]

The SK C/34 was effectively an improved version of the 11in. SK C/28 guns, which were the primary armament of the Deutschland-class cruisers and possessed a longer barrel. While the SK C/34 was of a smaller calibre than the main battery armaments of the capital ships in service with other navies, the 11in. weapon was preferred by a number of gunnery officers within the Kriegsmarine owing to the higher rate of fire offered.[4] While preferred by gunnery officers within the Kriegsmarine, the main factor behind the decision to arm the Scharnhorst-class with 11in. guns was political.

Since 1933 the commander-in-chief of the Reichsmarine, renamed in 1935 Kriegsmarine, Admiral Erich Raeder had argued for an increase in the offensive power of the *Panzerschiffe* design through the addition of a third turret. In 1934 Adolf Hitler, appointed chancellor the previous year, agreed to the adoption of a third turret in new designs.[5] When contracts were approved for the construction of two armoured ships in response to the construction of the Dunkerque-class by France's Marine Nationale, the main armament selected was 11in. guns. Some thought was given to arming the new ships with eight guns in two quadruple turrets, similar to the arrangement on the Dunkerque-class, however, this would have required a completely new design. Lengthy discussions were also held concerning the desirability of matching the 13in. armament of the French ships, with thought also being given to arming the new armoured ships with either 14in. or 15in. guns.[6] As had been the case with the idea to arm the ships with quadruple turrets, a completely new design would have been required.

At the same time, 14in. and 15in. guns would not have been approved by Hitler, who was anxious at the time for reconciliation with Great Britain. Opting for an armament of a calibre larger than 11in. risked jeopardising the negotiations which led to the Anglo-German Naval Agreement. Following the signing of the Anglo-German Naval Agreement on 18 June 1935, the original armoured ship design was scrapped with the decision being taken that the new ships should be capable of effectively countering the Dunkerque-class.

Under the terms of the Anglo-German Naval Agreement, the maximum gun calibre permitted was 16in. With this Hitler soon began to have second thoughts about the calibre of armament to be fitted to the new ships and ordered that they should be armed with 15in. guns. Such guns would take years to develop, while Hitler wanted capital ships as soon as possible, in order to implement his political ideas. At the same time Hitler was also reminded that while allowances were made under the terms of the Anglo-German Naval Agreement for a maximum gun calibre of 16in., Britain had historically been sensitive about increases in the main armament of German warships.[7] A compromise was therefore sought, with Hitler decreeing that the new design, which would become *Scharnhorst* and *Gneisenau*, would be armed with 11in. guns but that they would carry nine guns in three triple turrets. Hitler also decreed that the ships would be up-gunned to 15in. at the earliest opportunity.[8] The SK C/34

Ammunition, 11in., being hoisted aboard either *Scharnhorst* or *Gneisenau*. The ships were provided with three different types of shell including one armour-piercing type and two high-explosive shell types. All three types used the same propellant charges, a RPC/38 93.7-lb (42.5 kg) fore charge and a RPC/38 168.8-lb (76.5 kg) main charge. The SK C/34 that armed the Scharnhorst-class had a rate of fire of three shells per minute and each gun was expected to fire 300 rounds before enough wear had been incurred on the barrel to warrant replacement. (*Richard Aitken*)

guns of the Scharnhorst-class differed from earlier 11in. guns in possessing heavier shields, which were sometimes referred to as Drh LC/34.

The construction of the SK C/34 consisted on an 'A' tube with loose liner. A two-part jacket was shrunk over the 'A' tube for approximately two thirds of its length. On to the jacket, a breech end-piece was screwed on hot while the breech block supporting the piece screwed into the breech end pieces. The breech block was of a sliding type and weighted 0.98t. The loose liner weighed 6.6t and the 'A' tube 13.5t.[9] The guns were provided with three different type of shell, including a 727.5lb (330kg) armour piecing shell and two high explosive shell types, both of which weighed 694lb (315kg). All three types used the same propellant charges: a RPC/38 93.7lb (42.5kg) fore charge and a RPC/38 168.8lb (76.5kg) main charge. The SK C/34 that armed the Scharnhorst-class had a rate of fire of three shells/min. and each gun was expected to fire 300 rounds before enough wear had been incurred on the barrel to warrant replacement.

The guns were mounted in three Drh LC/34 turrets. The Drh LC/34 was essentially a replica of the Drh LC/28 turrets that housed the SK C/28 guns aboard the Deutschland-class. The main difference between the Drh LC/34 turrets of the Scharnhorst-class and the Drh LC/28 of the Deutschland-class was that the former were equipped with much stronger armour protection than the earlier model. Whereas the armour protection of the Drh LC/34 varied between 7.9in. and 14.2in., the armour of the Drh LC/28 of the Deutschland-class was 5.5in.

A propellant charge being loaded aboard *Scharnhorst*.

The forward 11in. guns of the *Gneisenau*. The ships of the Scharnhorst-class were armed with 11in. SK C/34 guns mounted in Drh LC/34 turrets. From bow to stern the turrets were known as 'Anton', 'Bruno' and 'Caeser'. (*NH 97538, US Naval History and Heritage Command Center*)

The turrets sat inside armoured barbettes on roller paths which were placed on top of support cylinders. The working levels of the turret revolved together and included the gun house, train mechanism level, machinery level, immediate level, propellant handling level and shell handling level. It may be noted that both the propellant handling level and the shell handling level were below the main armoured deck.[10]

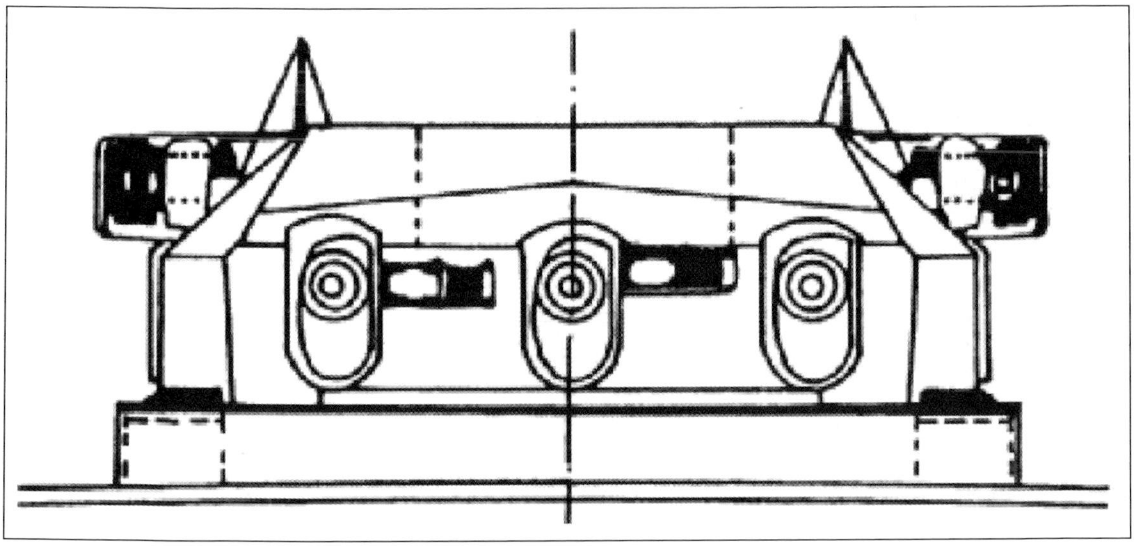

An illustration of the front of the main battery turrets of the Scharnhorst-class. (*Author's Collection*)

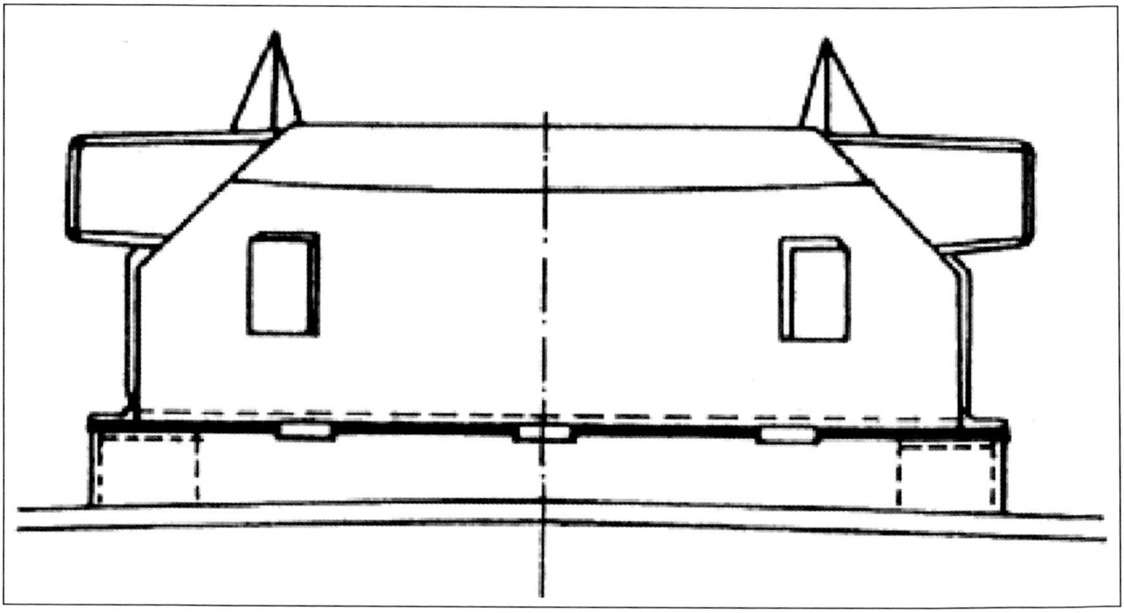

An illustration of the rear of the main battery turrets of the Scharnhorst-class. (*Author's Collection*)

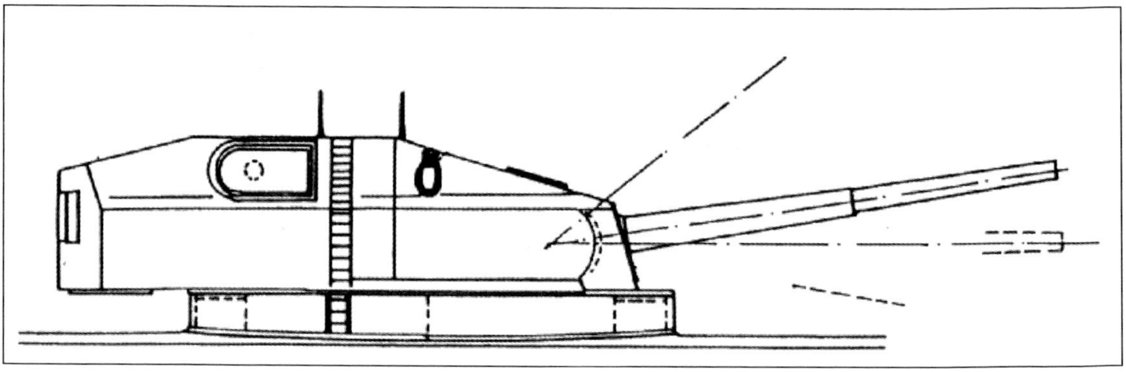

An illustration of the side of the main battery turrets of the Scharnhorst-class with gun elevations marked. (*Author's Collection*)

Upon sighting a target, the appropriate type of shell—armour piercing, high explosive nose fused, or high-explosive base fused—was selected and raised by hydraulic hoists from the shell room situated on the middle platform deck. At the same time the propellant charge, divided into the Vorkartuche fore charge housed within a silk bag, and the Hülsenkartuche main charge contained within a brass case, were placed next to the turret working levels. The charges were then raised by hydraulic hoists from their magazine on the upper platform deck. It may be noted that auxiliary hoists were provided for the turrets and that both the main hydraulic hoists and the auxiliary hoists could be operated manually in emergency situations. Transported up to the gun house,

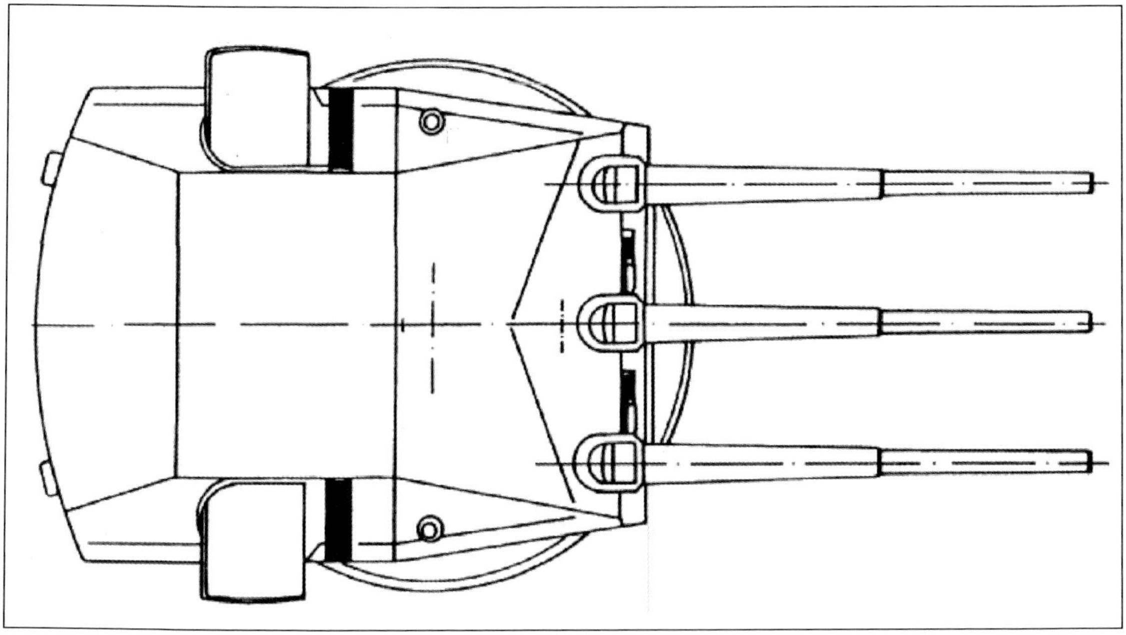

An illustration of the main battery turrets of the Scharnhorst-class viewed from above. (*Author's Collection*)

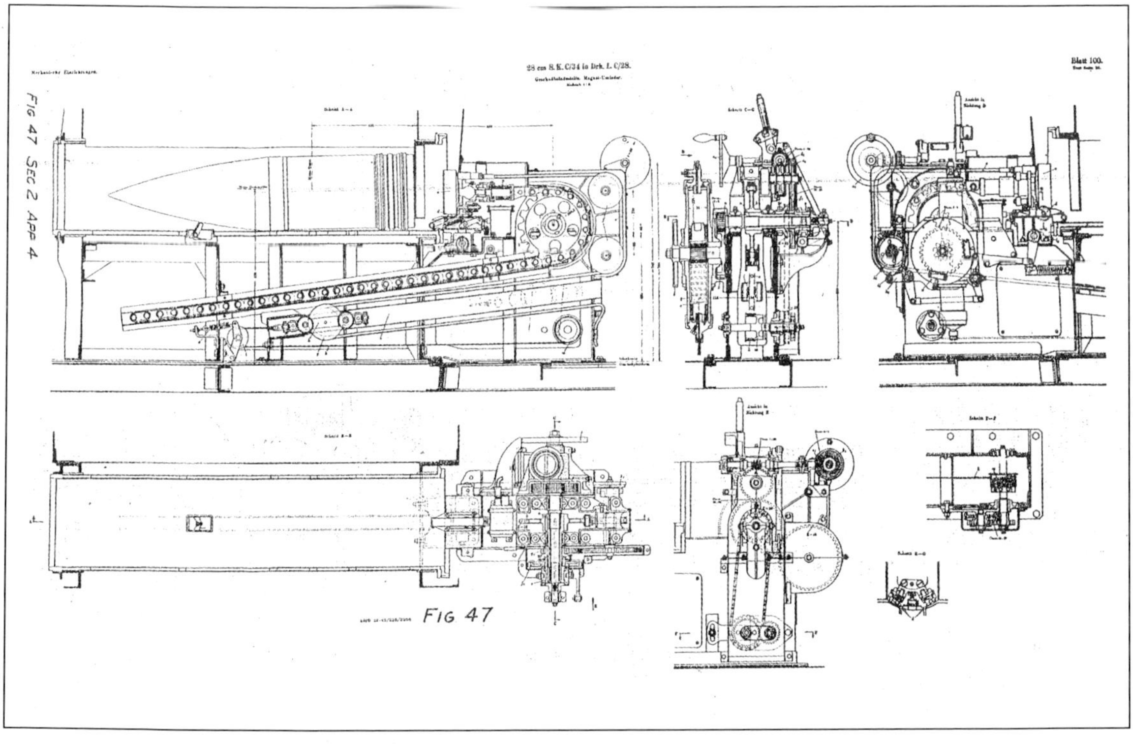

A drawing of the reloading mechanism of the Scharnhorst-class.

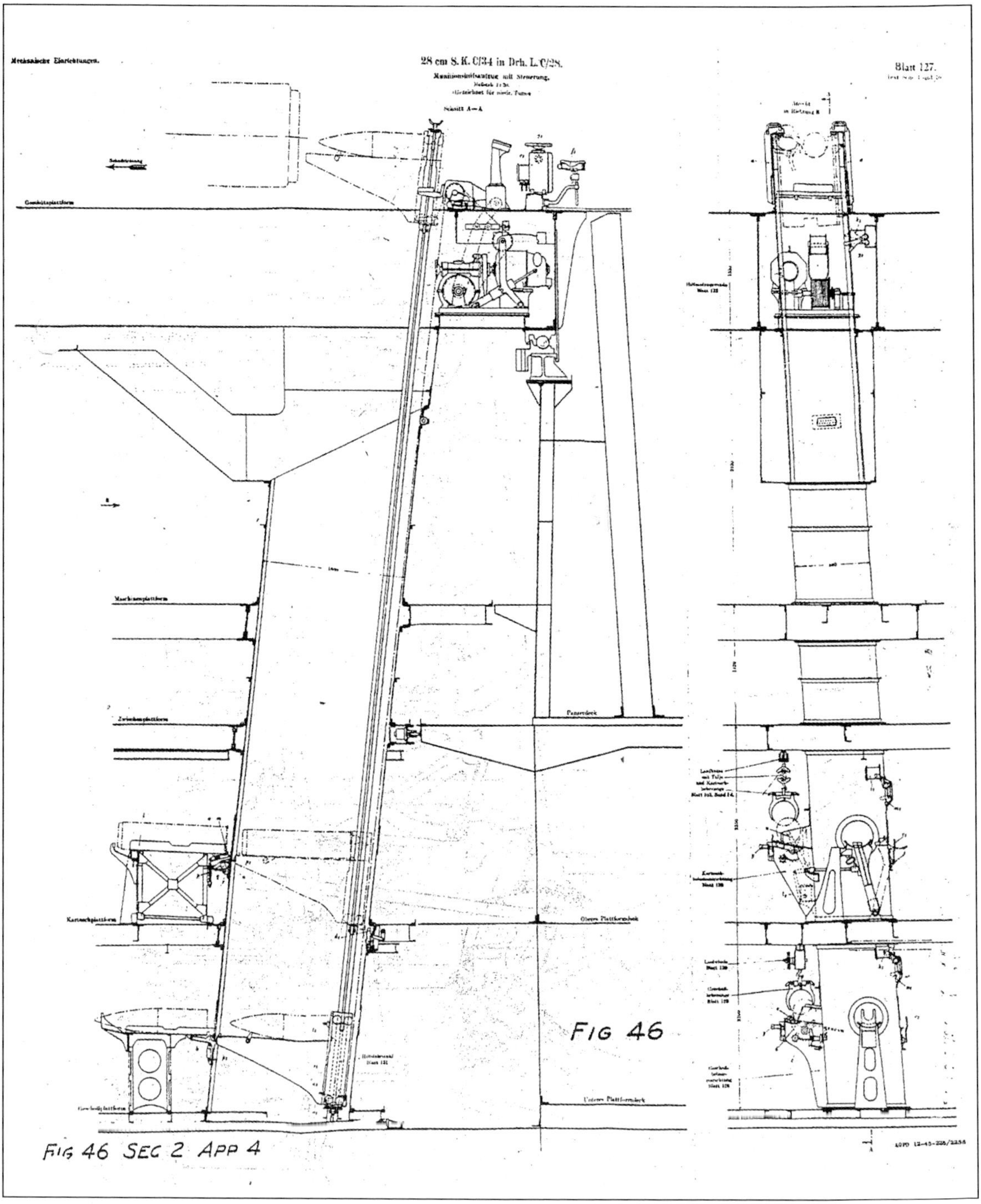

A drawing of the ammunition lift within the gun house of the Scharnhorst-class.

Turrets 'Anton' and 'Bruno' of *Scharnhorst* firing during the engagement which saw the sinking of HMS *Glorious* in 1940. When a full three gun salvo was fired by a turret, the central gun was delayed by approximately 20ms in order to minimise the effect of gun blast on the neighbouring gun barrels and to maintain a low dispersion. At maximum elevation, the SK C/34 guns fitted to the Scharnhorst-class were capable of hitting a target at a range of 25mi (40km). (*Gary Martin*)

Propellant cases on the deck of the *Scharnhorst* following the sinking of HMS *Glorious*. Having been fired, the empty propellant cases were ejected from the turret through openings in the gun-house floor located in the rear of the turret. Electric fans, meanwhile, extracted gases and smoke from the turret via ducts to exhausts located in the rear plate. (*Gary Martin*)

On the bow of the *Scharnhorst* looking aft during the winter of 1939–40, the guns of turret 'Anton' can be seen to be elevated almost to the maximum. The Drh LC/34 turrets had an electric system of operation with the elevation of the guns being provided by electric-driven hydraulic pumps. The turret could be traversed at a speed of 7.2°/s. The guns sited in turrets 'Anton' and 'Caesar' were capable of being elevated to 40° and depressed to -8°. The guns of turret 'Bruno', meanwhile, could be elevated to 40° and depressed to -9°. (*NH 101571, US History and Heritage Command*)

the shell and the propellant charges were loaded into the guns by telescopic chain rammers. Like the hoists, the telescopic chain rammers could be operated manually.[11]

When a full three gun salvo was fired by a turret, the central gun was delayed by approximately twenty milliseconds in order to minimise the effect of gun blast on the neighbouring gun barrels and to maintain a low dispersion. Having been fired, the empty propellant cases were ejected from the turret through openings in the gun house floor located in the rear of the turret. Electric fans, meanwhile, extracted gases and smoke from the turret via ducts to exhausts located in the rear plate.[12]

Similar to most other German installations, the Drh LC/34 turrets had an electric system of operation with the elevation of the guns being provided by electrically

General Characteristics	
Date of Design	*Date in Service*
1934	1938
Gun Weight	111,739.6lb (53,250kg)
Gun Length	58.58ft (17.85m)
Bore Length	47.57ft (14.50m)
Grooves	80
Rifling Length	38.45ft/461.6in. (11.72m)
Rate of Fire	3 rounds/min.
Mount	
Weight	165,467lb (750,000kg)
Elevation	–8°–+40° 'Anton' and 'Caesar' –9°–+40° 'Bruno'
Rate of Elevation	8°/s
Train	–150°–+150°
Rate of Train	7.2°/s
Loading Angle	2°
Ammunition	
Type	Cartridge bag
Projectile Type and Weight	Armour piercing 727.5lb (330kg) High-explosive nose fused 694.4lb (315kg) High-explosive base fused 694.4lb (315kg)
Bursting Charge	Armour piercing 14.55lb (7.84kg) High-explosive nose fused 48.06lb (21.8kg) High-explosive base fused 35.27lb (16kg)
Propellant Charge	Fore 93.7lb (42.5kg) RPC/38 Main 168.6lb (76.5kg) RPC/38
Muzzle Velocity	Armour piercing 2,920ft/s (890m/s)
Estimated Barrel Life	300 rounds

driven hydraulic pumps. It may also be noted that each of the guns had its own cradle and could be elevated independently of the others. The turrets could be traversed at a speed of 7.2°/sec. The guns sited in turrets 'Anton' and 'Caesar' were capable of being elevated to 40° and depressed to −8°. The guns of turret 'Bruno', meanwhile, could be elevated to 40° and depressed to −9°. For reloading, the guns had to be returned to an angle of 2°. At maximum elevation, the SK C/34 guns fitted to the Scharnhorst-class were capable of hitting a target at a range of 25mi (40km).[13]

According to design figures for the Scharnhorst-class, the ammunition stowage aboard the ships for each of the SK C/34 guns amounted to between 105 and 150 rounds.

The secondary armament of the Scharnhorst-class consisted of twelve 5.9in. (15cm) SK C/28 L/55 quick-firing guns. The design of the class allowed for a strong secondary armament battery as a means of defence against light enemy forces such as destroyers or torpedo boats. While the main armament was an improved version of the 11in. SK C/28 guns fitted to the Deutschland-class, when it came to the secondary armament, it was decided to use the successful 5.9in. (15cm) SK C/28 guns that had been fitted to the Deutschland-class as a secondary armament.[14]

The SK C/28 was designed as a smaller and lighter version of the 5.9in. (15cm) SK C/25 guns which had been used as the main armament aboard the ships of the Königsberg- and Leipzig-classes. The SK C/28, whilst featuring slight variations when compared to the SK C/25, was of a construction which resembled that of its predecessor, possessing a loose barrel, jacket and breech piece with a vertical sliding

The secondary armament of the Scharnhorst-class consisted of twelve 5.9in. (15cm) SK C/28 L/55 quick-firing guns. In the centre of this photograph taken aboard *Scharnhorst* are SK C/28 guns mounted in a Dopp LC/34 twin turret. Behind, a SK C/28 can be seen mounted in an MpL/35 pedestal mount. Also visible in the photograph are some of the ship's heavy anti-aircraft guns. (*NH 97507, US Naval History and Heritage Command Center*)

breech block.[15] The primary drawback of the SK C/28 was the fact that it was not a dual-purpose weapon, and could not serve in the anti-aircraft role. As the Second World War progressed, aircraft began to assert themselves as the primary threat to ships. This lack of a dual-purpose secondary armament put the ships of the Scharnhorst-class at odds with contemporary vessels such as the British King George V-class and the American North Carolina-class, which featured a secondary armament of dual-purpose guns.

The SK C/28 guns that were installed aboard the Scharnhorst-class were fitted into two different types of mountings. Eight of the guns were sited inside Dopp LC/34 twin turrets which were sited on both sides of the fore and aft superstructure. The remaining four guns were mounted individually in MpL/35 pedestal mounts which were sited amidships near the edge of the upper deck.[16] The Drh LC/34 turrets generally resembled the triple Drh LC/25 turrets used to mount the SK C/25 guns aboard the Leipzig-class and Königsberg-class cruisers. Internally, however, they were different. In the Drh LC/34 there was a double hoist between and at the rear of the guns which could simultaneously deliver two shells and two charges into the gun house for loading. In the Drh LC/34 mount the guns could be elevated to 40° and depressed to –10°.[17]

Scharnhorst at Wilhelmshaven in April 1939. The ship's 5.9in. SK C/28 guns in individual MpL/35 pedestal mounts can be seen. Four guns were mounted in such mounts aboard the Scharnhorst-class. (*World War Photos*)

A boatswain of the watch aboard *Scharnhorst* on duty amidships during the winter of 1939–40. One of the ship's SK C/28 guns can be seen in the background. (*NH 102533, US Naval History and Heritage Command Center*)

Gneisenau during Operation Berlin in 1941. One of the ship's 5.9in. turrets is in the foreground. (*NH 83099-KN, US Naval History and Heritage Command Center*)

General Characteristics	
Date of Design	*Date in Service*
1928	1934
Gun Weight	20,018lb (9,080kg)
Gun Length	26.91ft/323in. (8.2m)
Bore Length	25.64ft/307.7in. (7.81m)
Rifling Length	21.58ft/259in. (6.58m)
Rate of Fire	6 rounds/min.
Ammunition	
Projectile Type and Weight	Armour piercing 100.3lb (45.5kg) High-explosive base fuse 100.3lb (45.5kg) High-explosive nose fuse 98.5lb (44.7kg)
Bursting Charge	Armour piercing 2.91lb (1.32kg) TNT High-explosive base fuse 7.32lb (3.32kg) TNT High-explosive nose fuse 8.63lb (3.914kg) TNT
Propellant Charge	31.2lb (14.15kg) RPC/38
Cartridge Weight (empty)	18.83lb (8.54kg)
Muzzle Velocity	2,871ft/s 875m/s
Estimated Barrel Life	1,100 rounds
Ammunition Stowage Per Gun	113–150 rounds

Firing shells with a weight of 100lb (45.3kg), the guns at maximum elevation had a maximum firing range of 14mi (23km).[18] Each of the twin turrets was capable of firing up to six shells/min.[19] The MpL/35 mountings were based on the single MpL/28 mounts of the Deutschland-class. Where the two differed was in the gun shield. The gun shield of the MpL/35 was larger than that of the MpL/25, giving a total mounting weight of 26.29t (26,710kg) against 24.44t (24,830kg). In the MpL/35 mounting, the SK C/28 guns could be elevated to 35° and depressed to –10°.[20]

It is worth noting that while the SK C/28 was provided with three types of ammunition, the armour-piercing rounds were rarely carried. The magazines for the 5.9in. guns were situated below the armoured deck in sections VII and XIII. While ammunition hoists conveyed shells and cartridges from the magazines in the Drh LC/34 turrets, in the case of the MPL/35 mounts, the ammunition had to be manually carried to the guns from the hoists near the centreline.[21] The twin turrets had a training speed of 9°/s, while the single mounts had a training speed of 1.09°/sec. The guns, meanwhile, could be elevated at a speed of 8°/s.

Anti-aircraft defence was provided by three types of anti-aircraft gun. The heavy anti-aircraft armament of the Scharnhorst-class was provided by fourteen 4.1in. (10.5cm) SK C/33 L/65 guns. The SK C/33, which was used by the Kriegsmarine in the role of heavy anti-aircraft gun, was related to the 10.5cm Flak 38 anti-aircraft gun used by the Wehrmacht and would be mounted aboard the ships of the Scharnhorst-class as well as aboard the ships of the Bismarck-, Deutschland- and Admiral Hipper-classes.[22]

Sited in seven twin mounts, the weapons were all situated on the superstructure deck. Six of the mounts were symmetrically arranged around the funnel, while the seventh mount was to be found on the centreline in front of turret 'Caesar'. In their placement, the designers succeeded in providing the SK C/33 guns with very good arcs of fire; the only area with somewhat poor anti-aircraft cover by these guns was the area around the bow. The SK C/33 was composed of a loose barrel weighing 1.05t (1,075kg), a jacket, breech piece and vertical sliding breech block.[23] The SK C/33 guns were sited in Drh LC/31 mounts. The Drh LC/31 was an electrically powered tri-axial mounting that was designed to compensate for the movement of the ship and therefore allow the crew to remain accurately tracked on the target. The mounts were open to the weather and sea swell. Not correctly waterproofed, the SK C/33 guns proved to be a high maintenance burden.

The maximum firing range of the weapon was 7.08mi (11.39km), however, the effective range of the SK C/33 was 5.87mi (9.44km).[24] Capable of firing between

Crewmen aboard *Gneisenau* loading one of the ship's 4.1in. (10.5cm) SK C/33 L/65 guns. The Scharnhorst-class carried fourteen guns sited in Drh LC/31 mounts. (*NH 81940, US Naval History and Heritage Command Center*)

Likely taken from the superstructure aboard either *Gneisenau* or *Scharnhorst*, two of the ships SK C/33 L/65 anti-aircraft guns can be seen along with a single 5.9in. SK C/28 mount. The SK C/33 was related to the Flak 38 anti-aircraft gun used by the Wehrmacht and would be mounted aboard the ships of the Scharnhorst-class as well as the Bismarck-, Deutschland- and Admiral Hipper-classes. (*Beeldbank WO2*)

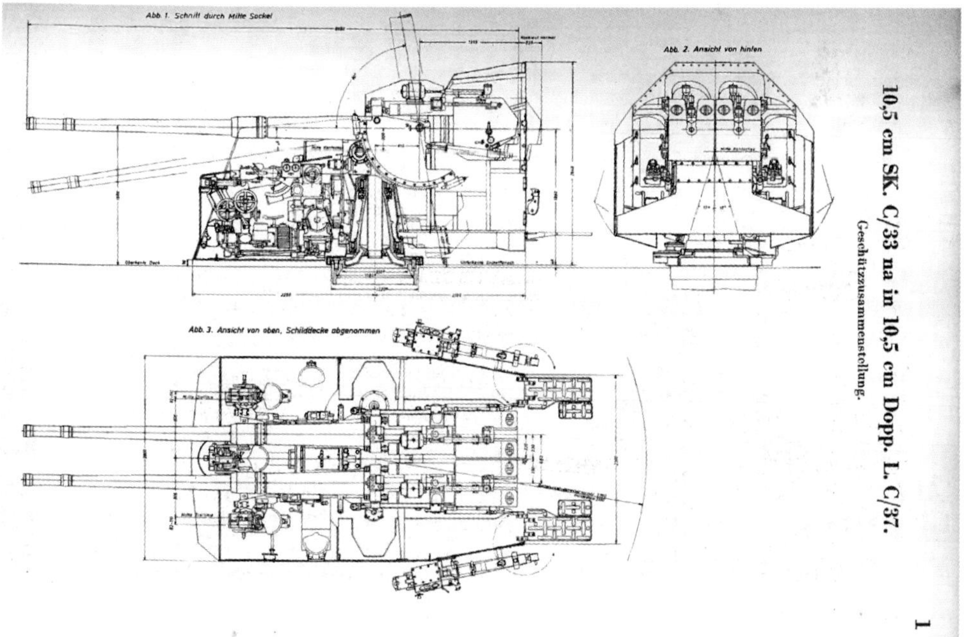

A dimensional drawing of an SK C/33.

fifteen and eighteen rounds/min., 400 rounds for each gun were stowed in the magazines. Fixed ammunition was fired by the gun, with the outfit of ammunition comprising nose-fused high explosive and high-explosive incendiary rounds.

The medium anti-aircraft armament of the Scharnhorst-class was provided by sixteen 1.47in. (3.7cm) SK C/30 guns. Mounted aboard every major German warship of the Second World War, the SK C/30 was a high-velocity semi-automatic weapon. While being a semi-automatic weapon, each shell was individually loaded, which meant that the SK C/30 was a slow-firing weapon for anti-aircraft defence. The SK C/30 guns were sited in eight twin mounts. Four of the mounts were sited on both sides of the aft superstructure. Forward, two mounts were sited on the lower mast deck level of the forward superstructure. This pair of mounts suffered from poor firing arcs. The final pair of mounts was to be found on the upper deck on both sides

Mounted aboard every major German warship of the Second World War, the SK C/30 was a high-velocity semi-automatic weapon. The example in this photograph was mounted aboard the training vessel *Drache*. While being a semi-automatic weapon, each shell was individually loaded, which meant that the SK C/30 was a slow-firing weapon for anti-aircraft defence. Aboard the Scharnhorst-class, the SK C/30 guns were mounted in the Drh LC/30 triaxially stabilised twin mount, which was produced by Rheinmetall. (*Bundesarchiv, Bild 101II-MN-0945-08*)

The medium anti-aircraft armament of the Scharnhorst-class was provided by sixteen 1.47in. (3.7cm) SK C/30 guns. In this photograph, a SK C/30 battery aboard *Gneisenau* is seen in action during firing exercises off Rügen Island, August 1939. (*Beeldbank WO2*)

of the superstructure. Initial operation of these two mounts proved troublesome with water pouring onto the deck in heavy weather. The situation was improved during the autumn of 1940 when new breakwaters were fitted in front of these gun mountings.[25]

The SK C/30 guns were mounted in the Drh LC/30 triaxially stabilised twin mount, which was produced by Rheinmetall. The Drh LC/30 was in essence a smaller version of the Drh LC/31 mounts which mounted the 4.1in. SK C/33 heavy anti-aircraft guns.[26] In the Drh LC/30 mount, the guns were mounted in separate cradles and were trained and elevated by hand, with direct gyro cross-levelling over 19.5°. The guns could be elevated to 85° and depressed to –9°.[27]

The light anti-aircraft armament of the class was made up of a number of 0.787in. (2cm) guns. Initially *Scharnhorst* and *Gneisenau* were provided with ten C/30 guns, which were manufactured by Rheinmetall. Mounted on single pedestal mounts on the upper deck and the superstructure, the C/30 was an automatic weapon but also prone to jamming. The guns were fed by a twenty-round magazine, which necessitated frequent pauses for reloading. In practical terms, this meant a poor rate of fire.

Aboard the ships of the Scharnhorst-class, the C/30 guns would be replaced in late 1940 and early 1941 by the new 0.787in. (2cm) C/38.[28] The C/38 was an improvement

Torpedo tubes aboard *Scharnhorst*. After 1942 six 21in. (53.3cm) deck-mounted torpedo tubes from the light cruisers *Leipzig* and *Nürnberg* were installed on the *Scharnhorst* and *Gneisenau*. The torpedo tubes were installed on the ships based on the recommendation of Admiral Günther Lütjens.

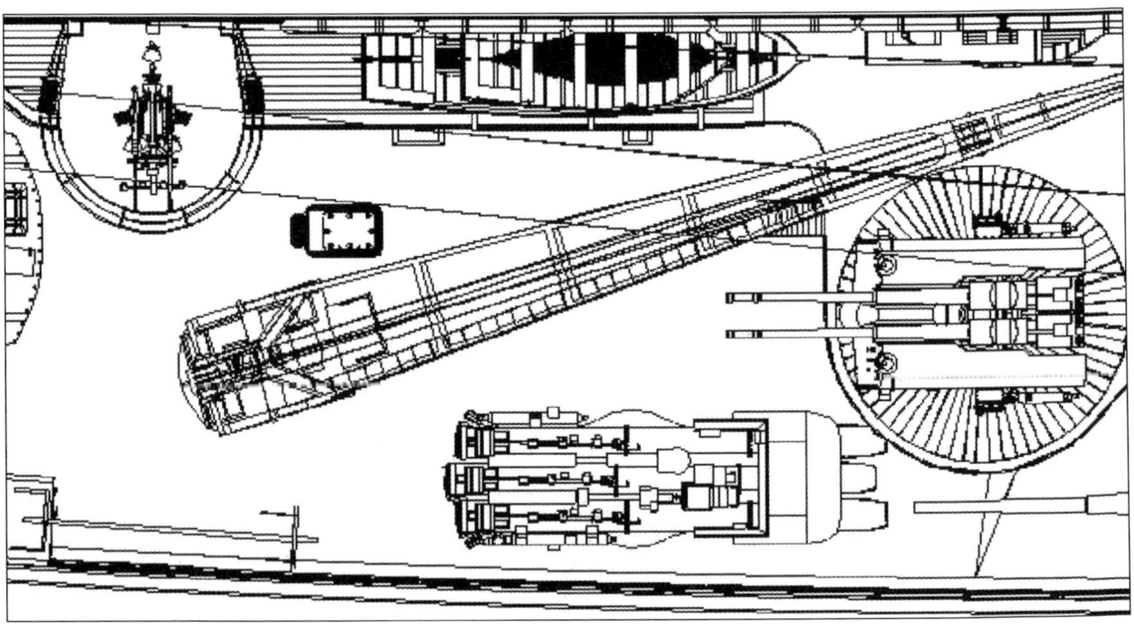

Amidships arrangement showing the location of the torpedo tubes.

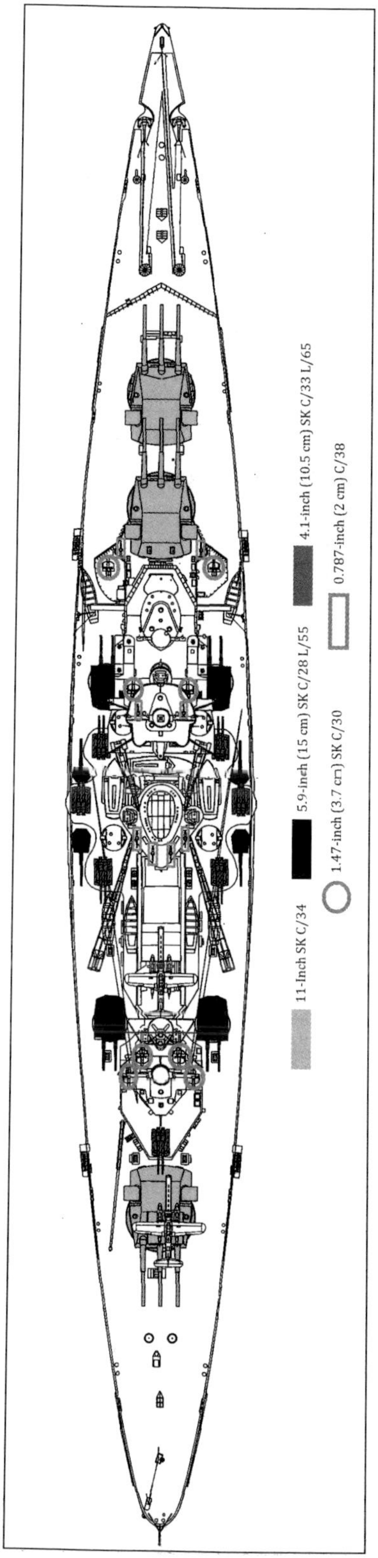

Scharnhorst-class armament layout, 1940. (*Author's Collection*)

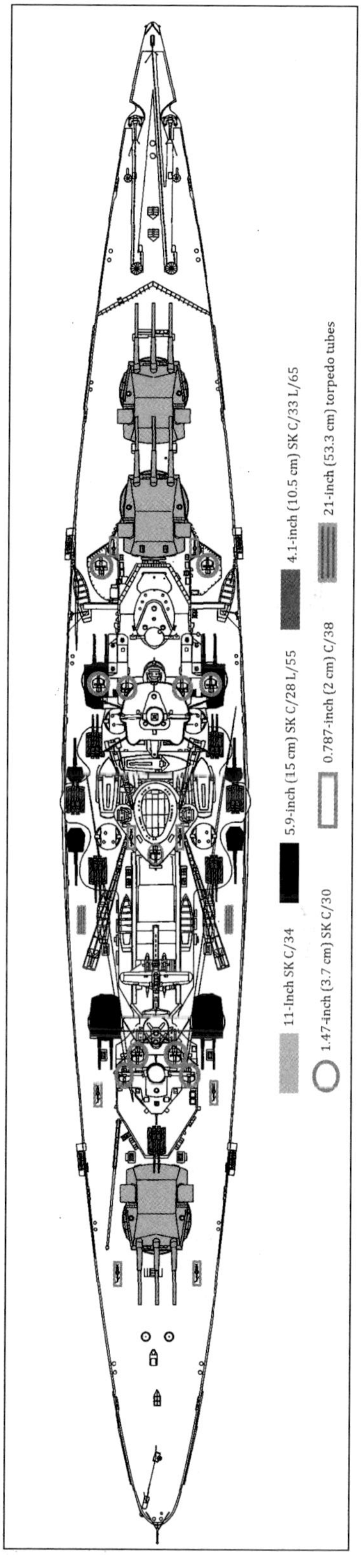

Scharnhorst-class armament layout, 1943. (*Author's Collection*)

on the C/30 and utilised a forty-round magazine. The C/38 would see service with the Wehrmacht as the 2cm Flak 38 and in the Flakvierling 38. Alongside the C/38, a new quadruple triaxially stabilised mount was developed. As the war progressed the C/38 armament would be incrementally increased. The guns were trained manually through the use of handwheels. The guns could be elevated up to 90° and depressed to −10°.[29] The C/38 had a theoretical rate of fire of 480 rounds/min., although 220 rounds/min. was the practical rate of fire.

After 1942 six 21in. (53.3cm) deck-mounted torpedo tubes from the light cruisers *Leipzig* and *Nürnberg* were installed on the *Scharnhorst* and *Gneisenau*. The torpedo tubes were installed on the ships beside the cranes amidships based on the recommendation of Admiral Günther Lütjens, who commanded the two ships during the Atlantic raiding sortie Operation Berlin between February and March 1941. Upon reaching Brest at the end of Operation Berlin, Lütjens put forward the recommendation that the ships should have a torpedo armament fitted because, in his view, too much time was often wasted in sending boarding parties or in using the primary or secondary armament to sink merchant ships. To Lütjens, a single torpedo fired from close range would be a more effective and quicker solution.[30]

The torpedo tubes launched the G7a T1 torpedo. Eighteen torpedoes could be stowed aboard each of the ships. The G7a T1 was a conventional wet-heater torpedo which could be set to run at one of three speeds: 30kt, 40kt or 44kt.[31] At 30kt, the torpedoes had a range of 8.69mi (13.9km). At 40kt the range of the torpedoes fell considerably to 4.97mi (8km), while when set to run at 44kt, the range of the weapon was 3.7mi (5.9km).[32] It was found that when set to run at 44kt ,the four-cylinder radial engine of the torpedo became overrated, which led to the 44kt setting being cancelled during the early years of the war. This setting would, however, later be reintroduced after engine modifications.[33] The G7a T1 torpedo, 23ft, 7in. (7.18m) long, was armed with a 661lb (300kg) Hexanite warhead.

In addition to the armament covered thus far, *Scharnhorst* was fitted with an additional armament not carried aboard *Gneisenau*: depth charges. Shortly before embarking upon Operation Berlin, two depth charge racks were fitted to *Scharnhorst* on the upper deck a short distance from the stern. Each rack carried three WBD depth charges. The effective use of the depth charges was very difficult owing to the limited manoeuvrability of the ship and would be removed in early 1942.

3

Hull Structure

The hulls of the ships of the Scharnhorst-class were constructed from longitudinal steel frames over which the outer hull plates were welded. The hulls contained twenty-one watertight compartments, while a double bottom covered approximately 80 per cent of their length.[1]

In the construction of the hull, two types of steel, ST 52 and ST 42, were used.[2] ST 52 is a low-carbon steel with manganese content. Possessing good impact resistance and material strength, ST52 possesses good structural hardness and is considered quite ductile, meaning that it can be plastically reformed into the required shapes without any need for heat treatment. ST 42 is a steel generally used in the construction of structures where fatigue, wide fluctuations of stress and reversals of stress are involved. This tends to see ST 42 used in such things a girders.

The hull was almost entirely welded, with rivets only being used in the most critical joints between the armour plates. The ships of the Scharnhorst-class were amongst the first capital ships in the world whose construction integrated welding to such a large extent, allowing for significant weight savings.[3]

As previously noted, internally the ships were divided into twenty-one watertight compartments, the compartments being divided by transverse bulkheads. The watertight compartments were designated by Roman numerals, with compartment XXI at the bow and compartment I at the stern.[4] Frame 0 marked the aftermost point of the waterline, with frame 226, when the ships were completed, forming the bow. When the bow of the two ships was rebuilt and the straight stems were replaced by the Atlantic bow, several more frames were added to the hull structure.

Considered to be poor sea boats, the Scharnhorst-class were bow heavy when at full load and were wet as high as the bridge in heavy seas, with turret 'Anton' suffering from flooding. Having originally been completed with a straight stem, the seakeeping of both ships was improved somewhat with the replacement of the straight stem with the flared Atlantic bow. The Atlantic bow allowed the ships to gain more freeboard and sheer, and increased the lift ability of the bow. *Gneisenau* would be taken in hand in October 1938 for a number of modifications, including the replacement of the bow, while *Scharnhorst* was taken in hand in July 1939 specifically for bow replacement.[5]

The launch of the *Scharnhorst* at the Kriegsmarinewerft, Wilhelmshaven, 3 October 1936. Prior to being launched, the hull spent sixteen months on the slipway. Here the bow has been completed with a straight stem. (*World War Photos*)

The hull of the *Gneisenau* shortly before being launched on 8 December 1936 at the Deutsche Werke, Kiel. As with *Scharnhorst*, *Gneisenau* was completed with a straight stem which would later be replaced by an Atlantic bow. (*NH 110878, US Naval History and Heritage Command Center*)

Scharnhorst (left) and *Gneisenau* (right) alongside in a German port during the spring or early summer of 1939. At the time that this photograph was taken, *Gneisenau* had been refitted with an Atlantic bow, while *Scharnhorst* was yet to be similarly fitted. (*NH 97537, US Naval History and Heritage Command Center*)

Taken prior to the outbreak of war, here the *Gneisenau* is photographed at anchor in Madeira. This photograph illustrates well the Atlantic bow fitted to the ship. (*Author's Collection*)

Scharnhorst photographed at the beginning of July 1939, having been taken in hand in the 40,000t floating dry dock at the Westwerft for a refit which saw the straight stem replaced by an Atlantic bow. (*Author's Collection*)

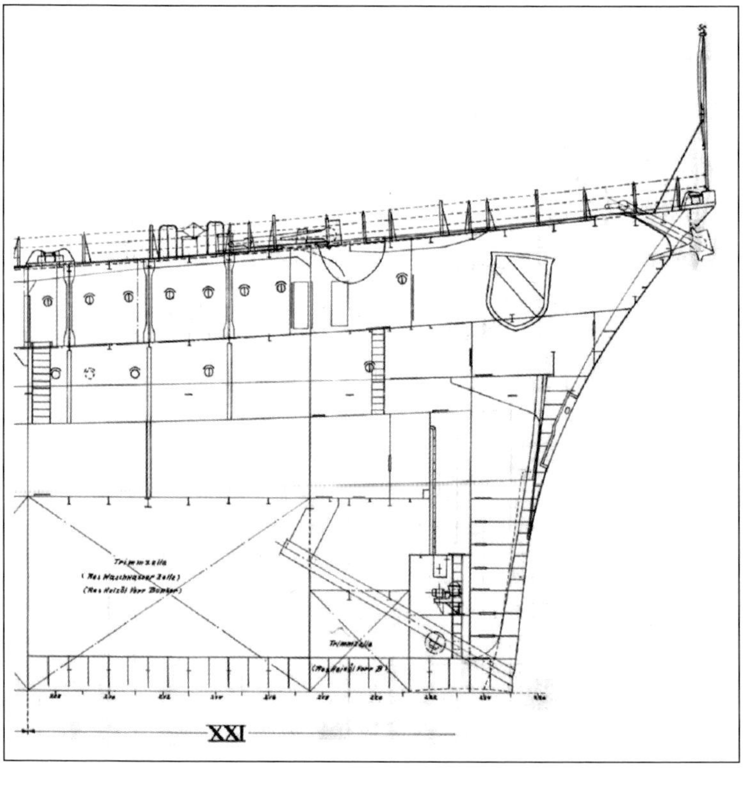

Section XXI from an original German plan dated 1939 showing the bow area of the *Scharnhorst*.

Taken during the commissioning ceremony of the *Scharnhorst* on 7 January 1939, this photograph provides a detailed view of the stern, including the bronze eagle fitted to the stern. Like the forecastle, the stern of the ships of the Scharnhorst-class was also frequently wet. (*NH 97536, US Naval History and Heritage Command*)

Taken while alongside in Brest following Operation Berlin, this photograph offers a stern view of a weather-beaten *Scharnhorst*. (*Author's Collection*)

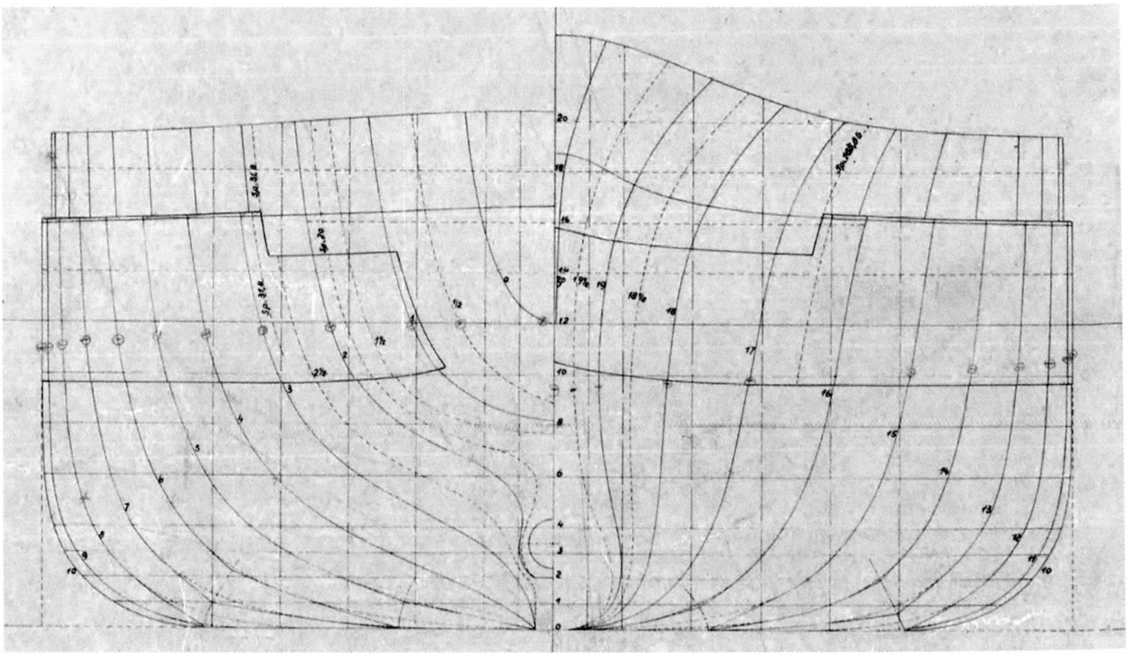

Bow and stern technical drawings of the Scharnhorst-class.

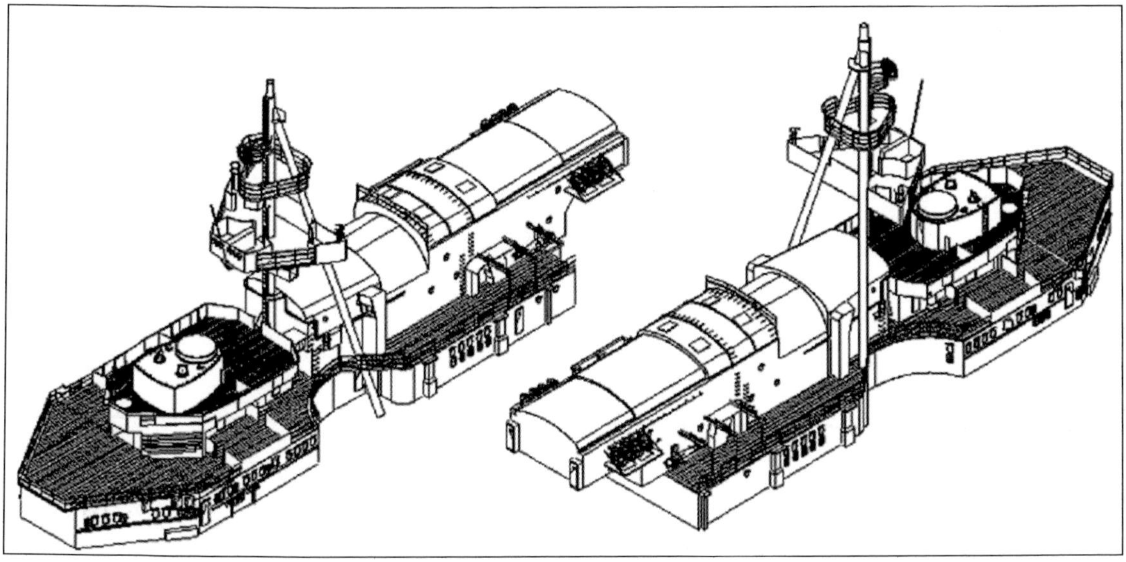

An illustration of the aft superstructure of the *Scharnhorst*.

The stern of the ships of the Scharnhorst-class was also frequently wet, and the ships were somewhat sluggish when entering a turn. In shallow water, the handling and response to the helm of both ships was considered so poor that they almost always required the assistance of tug boats.[6]

The double bottom, comprising frames 21–229, had a height of 5ft, 5in. (1.7m). The inside spaces of the double bottom were used to store fuel oil and water.[7] While the dense division of compartments gave *Scharnhorst* and *Gneisenau* the capability of remaining afloat with significant damage, the stability of the ships was further improved by fitting a pair of bilge keels between frames 75 and 143.

4

Armour

The designers of the Scharnhorst-class placed an emphasis on providing the ships with a strong armour arrangement. To provide protection, the ships of the class were equipped with Krupp armour. As such three types of armour were used on the ships: Krupp cementite, Wotan hart [hard] and Wotan weich [soft]. Krupp Cementite was a face-hardened armour steel. The outer layer of Krupp cementite was extremely hard, reaching 670 on the Brinell scale. The hardness decreased through the depth of the plate in order to prevent cracking when hit by a projectile. This type of armour was used for most of the vertical armour plate, including the armour belt, the fore and aft armoured bulkheads, and the conning tower as well as in the turrets and barbettes.[1]

Wotan hart was a homogenous armour steel characterized by its tensile strength of 85–96kg/mm^2, strain of 20 per cent and yield point of 50–55kg/mm^2.[2] Wotan hart armour would be used for the side armour plates fore and aft of the citadel and for the armoured deck plates. Wotan weich was another homogenous armour steel. It had a tensile strength of 65–75kg/mm^2, a strain of 25 per cent and a yield point of 38–40kg/mm^2.[3] Wotan weich armour would be used in the Scharnhorst-class for the longitudinal torpedo bulkheads. In the construction of the ships of the Scharnhorst-class, both Wotan hart and Wotan weich would be used extensively, for the first time in a German warship.

The ships of the Scharnhorst-class had an armoured deck which was 2in. (50mm) thick. The armoured deck was, in turn, backed by the main armour deck. The main armour deck was 0.79in. (20mm) thick at the bow and increased to 2in. in the central portion of the ship which contained the machinery spaces and magazines, before decreasing to 0.9in. aft.[4] In this layout, the armoured deck was intended to de-cap and set off the fuse of the incoming shell and reduce the chance of a shell penetrating the main armour deck and detonating in the machinery spaces. This layout was, however, controversial, as two separate decks offered less resistance to both projectiles and bombs than would have been offered by one thicker deck of the same combined weight.

The main armoured deck covered most of the length of the ships and was supported by 4.1in. (105mm) thick slopes on either longitudinal side.[5] These slopes connected to the lower edge of the main belt and served to significantly increase the armour protection over the vital areas of the ship. This arrangement of a flat centreline with outboard slopes was referred to as a 'turtle back'.[6]

The key element of the armour layout of the Scharnhorst-class was the citadel, an armoured box without a base. The citadel covered the most vital areas of the ship, in particular the magazines and the machinery spaces in hull sections III through XVIII. The concept behind the citadel design of the Scharnhorst-class was the belief that engagements would likely be fought at relatively short ranges owing to the poor visibility typical of the North Atlantic. As such, emphasis was placed on protecting the ships from horizontal fire as opposed to plunging fire.[7] Indeed, the Scharnhorst-class were well armoured against any calibre of shell fired by battleships of the time at shorter ranges.[8]

The belt armour of the Scharnhorst-class was composed of Krupp cemented steel armour and was 14in. thick in the central portion of the ship where the vital areas were located.[9] Towards the bow and stern the armoured belt inclined outwards, which served to increase resistance.[10] Forward of turret 'Anton' the belt armour tapered to 5.9in. before tapering to nothing at the bow. Aft of turret 'Caesar' the belt armour decreased to 7.9in., before tapering away to nothing at the stern. While extending from the front of the magazines for turret 'Anton' and to the rear of the magazine for turret 'Caesar', the armour belt was 14ft, 7in. (4.5m) high. The central portion of the belt was backed by 6.7in.-thick shields.[11] Between the armoured belt and the hull plating was fitted a shock-absorbing layer of teak wood.

The best-protected part of the Scharnhorst-class was the forward conning tower. The roof of the conning tower was 7.9in. thick, while the side walls were 13.7in. thick, tapering to 2.3in. below the level of the bridge deck. The communications shaft was protected by 8.6in. thick plating. The main fire-control position could not be afforded extensive armour protection owing to its position high above the waterline. The sides of the main fire-control position were 2.3in. thick, while the roof was a mere 1.1in. thick.[12] While the forward conning tower was the best protected area of the ship, the rear coning tower of the Scharnhorst-class was considerably less so, possessing sides which were 3.9in. thick and a roof 2in. thick.[13] The communications shaft in the aft conning tower was afforded 1.9in. of protection. The three rangefinders fitted aboard the ships were also provided with armour plating. The fore rangefinder was equipped with a 3.9in.-thick roof and 7.8in.-thick sides. The main rangefinder had a 1.1in.-thick roof and sides, while the aft rangefinder had a 1.9in.-thick roof and 3.9in.-thick sides.[14]

The barbettes which housed the main battery turrets were heavily armoured with Krupp cemented steel. The sides of the barbettes were 13.7in. thick and tapered to 7.9in. on the centreline, where they were shielded by the gun turrets above.[15] The main battery turrets themselves were extensively protected. The face of the turrets was protected by 14.1in. of armour plating, while the sides were 7.8in., tapering to 4.3in. The rear of the turrets was protected by 6.6in. of armour, while their roofs were protected by 5.9in. of armour at their thickest, tapering to 3.5in. The secondary armament turrets were also afforded armour protection. The face of the turrets were provided with 5.5in. of armour, while the sides and rear of the turrets were 2.3in. thick. The roof of the turrets was comprised of a fore and aft plate. The fore roof plate was 1.9in. thick, while the aft roof plate was 1.1in. thick. The barbettes of the secondary armament were protected by 5.9in. of armour.[16]

This photograph shows *Scharnhorst* whilst undergoing fitting-out work in 1937. Turret 'Anton' has been mounted. Behind, the barbette of turret 'Bruno' can be seen, minus the turret, along with the raw structure of the armoured bridge. The barbettes which housed the main battery turrets were heavily armoured with Krupp cemented steel. The sides of the barbettes were 13.7in. thick and tapered to 7.9in. on the centreline, where they were shielded by the gun turrets above. (*Author's Collection*)

The underwater protection system of the Scharnhorst-class was designed to withstand a direct hit from a 550lb explosive warhead. During the interwar period, the Reichsmarine had conducted several full-scale underwater explosion tests with sections of armour cut from the pre-dreadnought battleship *Preussen*, the results of which informed the design of the underwater protection system. The tests revealed that a welded construction better withstood the impact of a 550lb warhead than did a riveted construction.

The torpedo bulkhead of the ships was composed of Wotan weich steel placed behind the armoured belt, which was riveted. This was done because plate joints which had been incorrectly welded would not sufficiently withstand the explosive shocks of a torpedo impact and detonation.[17]

The underwater protection system was composed of several layers. The outer layer, which varied between 0.47 and 2.6in. in thickness, was located directly underneath the main armour belt and was designed to detonate a torpedo warhead. Behind the outer plate was a large void that had been incorporated so as to allow gases from the explosion to expand and dissipate. Beyond this void was a fuel bunker complete with a 0.31in. thick outer wall designed to absorb any remaining explosive force. The fuel bunker was supported by longitudinal stiffeners and transverse bulkheads.[18]

The underwater side protection system did, however, possess a number of faults. While the system was extremely strong amidships, at either end of the citadel it was significantly weaker. This meant that, while a 550lb warhead could be withstood amidships, at the ends of the citadel the side protection system was only sufficient to withstand a 440lb warhead. A further significant weakness in the design was the arrangement of the torpedo bulkhead. The torpedo bulkhead was connected to the lower portion of the sloped deck at an angle of 10° and was held in place by two riveted angled bars. The bars were constantly placed under a significant amount of stress owing to the bending forces of the hull. When combined with the explosive force of a torpedo warhead, the bars could not withstand the increased pressure and were likely to fail. Finally, the beam of the ships, at 98.5ft (30m), meant that the underwater protection system had to be weaker around the main battery turrets as a significant amount of hull space around the main armament was taken up by the barbettes and magazines.[19]

Armour arrangement of the Scharnhorst-class. (*Author's Collection*)

5

Propulsion

During the initial designs it was intended that the ships of the Scharnhorst-class would be provided with a diesel propulsion system, as a diesel system had been used successfully in the Deutschland-class *Panzerschiffe*. It was, however, ultimately decided to equip the ships of the Scharnhorst-class with a superheated steam propulsion system because the total output required to achieve the desired speed of the class was three times that of the power output of the Deutschland-class. In the case of a triple-screw vessel this would have meant more than twice the shaft horsepower per shaft of the Deutschland-class, while in the case of a ship with quadruple screws, this would have amounted to more than 40,000 horsepower per shaft.[1] This was a requirement beyond the diesel technology available at the time, and devising and producing engines which could have met this demand would have taken up an unforeseen amount of time. As high-pressure superheated steam had already proved to be a successful method of propulsion, it was considered the most suitable choice for high-power machinery.[2]

Scharnhorst was powered by three Brown, Boveri, & Co. geared steam turbines, while *Gneisenau* was powered by three Germania geared turbines.[3] In order to drive the turbines, steam was required. Twelve Wagner high-pressure steam-heated boilers with natural water circulation were fitted to the ships in the boiler rooms. Each of the boiler rooms contained three boilers. In each of the boiler rooms was a boiler drum, each of which was connected to two Saake burners at one end.

Each boiler was manufactured by Deschimag, Bremen and had an evaporation heating surface of 4,574.66ft^2 (425m^2), a superheater heating surface of 1,399.3ft^2 (130m^2) and an air pre-heat surface of 8,611.13ft^2 (800m^2). The boilers were capable of producing 54t of steam per hour and had an operating pressure of 50atm. The operating temperatures of the saturated steam produced by the boilers was 263°C and 480°C for superheated steam.[4] Each boiler had a height of 21.6ft (6.59m), which forced the designers to raise the ceiling of the boiler rooms by 19.6in. (50cm) above the original design and produced a discontinuity in the armour arrangement.[5] In addition to the three boiler rooms, the Scharnhorst-class were equipped with an auxiliary boiler room located in section XIII, used mainly whilst in harbour.[6]

From the boiler rooms, steam was piped into the turbine rooms. Each of the geared turbines was comprised of a high-pressure turbine rated at 5,100rpm, a low-pressure turbine rated at 3,1600rpm and an immediate pressure turbine rated at 3,150rpm.

A crew member at work in the engine room of the *Scharnhorst*. *Scharnhorst* was powered by three Brown, Boveri, & Co. geared steam turbines while *Gneisenau* was powered by three Germania geared turbines. (*Peter Moise*)

The engine room of the *Scharnhorst*. (*Author's Collection*)

In addition to these, the ships were fitted with a high-pressure astern turbine, a low-pressure astern turbine and a cruising turbine.[7]

The turbine turning gear was situated behind the centrally located couplings and a high-pressure bearing. When not in use, changes in temperature could have an adverse effect upon the turbine motors. As such, after a turbine had been shut down following a period of being underway, the installation had to be regularly rotated until it had cooled to the surrounding air temperature. In harbour this was undertaken once daily.[8] The cruising turbine of the ships was a Curtis wheel with four single states. During sea trials the cruising turbine aboard both the *Scharnhorst* and *Gneisenau* was found to be unsatisfactory and would eventually be discarded.[9] The turbines of the ships drove three shafts attached to three-blade screws, each of which was 15ft, 9in. (4.8m) in diameter.

To fuel the boilers, the bunkers of the ships could carry 2,800t of fuel oil as designed, though additional storage areas were also utilised, including hull spaces between the belt armour and the torpedo bulkhead, serving to increase the capacity of the ships to 6,200t. The propulsion system of the Scharnhorst-class was designed to give an output of 125,000shp. On trials, however, *Scharnhorst* developed an output of 160,050shp. *Gneisenau*, by contrast, developed only 109,000shp during trials over a measured mile shortly after entering commission, although it may be noted that on later trials she developed an output of 154,000shp.[10] The designed speed of the class was 31kt. Both vessels would exceed the designed speed, with *Scharnhorst* attaining 31.65kt and *Gneisenau* 31.3kt. At maximum fuel load, the ships were expected to be able to sail 9,300mi (15,000km) at a cruising speed of 19kt. In actuality, however, *Scharnhorst* would capable of sailing 8,200mi (13,100km) at 19kt. while *Gneisenau* was capable of sailing only 7,100mi (11,500km) at the same speed.[11]

Every engine type has its pros and cons. Diesel engines are immediately ready to provide drive and can immediately be put to maximum revolutions from zero. With steam systems like those fitted aboard the Scharnhorst-class, much more time is required. From cold, when all of the boilers have been shut down and none of the turbines have been pre-heated, it can take up to two hours before the turbines are sufficiently pressurised to begin to provide drive. In addition to this, diesel systems are generally more economical. For this reason the Deutschland-class cruiser *Admiral Graf Spee* would be able to target merchant shipping in the South Atlantic and Indian Ocean, covering vast distances between rendezvous with her supply ship *Altmark* during the first few months of the Second World War, while the *Scharnhorst* and *Gneisenau* with their steam turbines were confined to the North Atlantic.

In terms of maximising space, a steam plant is more advantageous when compared to a diesel propulsion system. The high output required of diesel turbines demands several motors which take up a significant amount of floor space, whereas the high-pressure steam turbines of the Scharnhorst-class required much less space.[12]

A post-war memorandum written by Ludwig Cordes, a noted authority on the German navy, made the point:

> When war broke out in 1939 it was clear that the majority of warships either in commission or building, and especially the larger surface units, were not suitable for the war at sea against enemy commerce irrespective of whether the enemy was

> Poland, France or Britain. This had been a lesson of the First World War which should logically have been taken to heart when rebuilding the Fleet. In fact it had been one of the decisive lessons of the First World War that the German High Seas Fleet, though outstanding technically, was so limited in its range as to present no effective threat to Britain's lines of supply.
>
> When rebuilding the Fleet, the dictum to have been borne in mind when planning any German surface warship was 'great range'. This had been realised in 1928 when the *Deutschland* class Panzerschiffe were designed with diesel drive. All the more incomprehensible, then, was the reversion in 1934 to steam-driven battleships such as *Scharnhorst* and *Gneisenau*, and later *Bismarck* and *Tirpitz*. This cut the 20,000nm radius of action of the armoured ships to less than half that for battleships. It was in that fact that the German surface navy ceased to be an effective opposition to any sea power.[13]

The *Scharnhorst* and *Gneisenau* were very much products of their time. After the First World War the Reichsmarine had little opportunity to carry out a thorough and

A close-up of the funnel area amidships of *Scharnhorst* before the ship underwent a refit in 1939.

Scharnhorst alongside during the launching ceremony of the *Tirpitz*. Note the flat funnel cap.

Gneisenau underway, 1938. Note the smoke and exhaust gases from the funnel. This photograph was taken prior to the installation of the raked funnel cap, which was intended to direct smoke and exhaust gases away from the deck and forward superstructure. (*World War Photos*)

intensive programme of experiments aimed at developing such things as diesel drive, which could have potentially prevented a reversion to steam propulsion.

The exhaust gases from the boilers and engines were vented upwards through the funnel. Originally the ships of the Scharnhorst-class were completed with a flat funnel cap, which would later be modified to a raked funnel cap. The modifications to the funnel were made when the straight stems of *Scharnhorst* and *Gneisenau* were replaced with the Atlantic bow, and also saw the main mast moved aft. The raked funnel cap was intended to direct smoke and exhaust gases away from the deck and forward superstructure.

Scharnhorst, early autumn 1939, following the completion of her refit. Note the ship has been fitted with a raked funnel cap. (*NH 101558, US Naval History and Heritage Command Center*)

The view from the foretop of the *Scharnhorst* looking down at the base of the funnel. Note the crewmen working on what appears to be a paravane at the bottom of the image. (*NH 102545, US Naval History and Heritage Command Center*)

6

Electrical Power

A sufficient amount of electrical power was required to power systems across the ships, the most important of which were the main battery and the fire-control drives, the ammunition hoists, steering, pumps and the lighting onboard as well as the communication and ventilation systems. In addition to this, redundancy was also required. In order to meet the electricity demands, the Scharnhorst-class were provided with five electricity plants, which gave a total power output of 4,120kW at 210V.[1]

In electrical generator room I, situated in section IV on the port side, two steam generators were located, which had an individual output of 240 kw. Electrical generator room II was situated in section IX on the starboard side and was also equipped with two steam generators. Each of the generators had an output of 460kW.[2] Electrical generator room III was situated in section XI on the port side and contained two steam generators with an individual output of 460kW. Electrical generator room IV in section XII on the starboard side contained a further two steam generators with an individual output of 460kW. Electrical generator room V located in section XIII on the port side contained two steam generators and two diesel generators. Each of the steam generators had a power output of 300kW, while the diesel generators each had a power output of 150kW.[3]

7

Radar and Rangefinders

Both ships of the Scharnhorst-class were equipped with Seetakt radar sets. During the late 1920s, Hans Hollmann began work in the field of microwaves, which was to become the basis of most radio-direction finding or radar systems. In 1935 Hollmann published a work titled *Physics and Technique of Ultrashort Waves*. This work was picked up by researchers around the globe. At the time of the book's writing and publication, Hollmann had been interested in the use of microwaves for communication. At the same time, however, Hollmann and his partner, Hans-Karl von Willisen, also began work on radar-like systems.[1]

In 1928 Hollmann and von Willisen, together with Paul-Günther Erbslöh, established a company called Gesellschaft für Elektroakustische und Mechanische Apparate, also known by the acronym GEMA.[2] In the autumn of 1934, GEMA constructed the first commercial radar system for use in detecting ships. The system developed by GEMA was similar to that developed by Christian Hülsmeyer, who in 1904 had given public demonstrations in Germany and in the Netherlands of the use of radio echoes to detect ships and avoid collisions. Hülsmeyer's system consisted of a simple spark gap used to generate a signal that was aimed using a dipole antenna with a cylindrical parabolic reflector. When a signal was reflected from a ship, it was picked up by a similar antenna attached to a separate coherer receiver. The system was capable of picking up the presence of ships at a range of 1.8mi (3km). Hülsmeyer's system did not provide range data, rather it merely provided warning of a nearby object.

The system constructed by GEMA, like the Hülsmeyer system, only provided a warning that a ship was in the general vicinity of the direction that the radar antenna was pointing and did not provide an accurate direction of travel or any information relating to the range of the vessel. Operating in the 50cm range, the system could detect ships up to 6.2mi (10km) away.

During the summer of 1935, on orders from the Kriegsmarine, GEMA developed a pulse radar system which successfully detected the cruiser *Königsberg* at a range of 5mi (8km) and had an accuracy of up to 54.6yds (50m). The same system could detect an aircraft at an altitude of 1,640ft (500m) at a range of 17.3mi (28km).[3] The military implications of the system were not lost in German military circles, with work beginning on both sea- and land-based variants of the system. The land-based variant was known as Freya radar while the sea-based variant was designated Seetakt.

The priority of the Kriegsmarine at the time was for a system which could be used for ranging. Detecting targets and objects at night or in poor visibility was of secondary importance. Even radar for use in gun laying was not a priority for the Kriegsmarine.

Early Seetakt systems worked on a 50cm (600MHz) wavelength. but these proved problematic and quickly led to the development of a new version which possessed improved electronics and worked on a 60cm (500MHz) wavelength. Four units were ordered, with the first being installed upon the Deutschland-class cruiser *Admiral Graf Spee* in January 1938. The other three units were installed on two large torpedo boats and on the Königsberg-class light cruiser *Königsberg*. The Seetakt system mounted aboard the *Admiral Graf Spee*, *Königsberg* and the two torpedo boats operated on 500MHz, while the maximum range at which a ship-sized target could be detected was 100mi (220km) under perfect conditions. Typically, however, the detection of a ship-sized target was approximately 50mi (80.4km).

The early model Seetakt systems were, in 1939, followed by a modified version known as DeTe 1. The DeTe 1 version of Seetakt operated between 368MHz and 390MHz. On the battleships of the Scharnhorst-class, one Seetakt set was mounted on the forward main battery director, which was mounted on top of the bridge, while the second radar set was mounted on the aft main battery director. The Seetakt sets

The forward armament of the *Gneisenau*, c. 1940. Note the FuMO 22 radar atop the director tower. (*NH 81941, US Naval History and Heritage Command Center*)

fitted to the Scharnhorst-class operated initially at 368MHz at 14kW. The sets would later be upgraded to 375MHz at 100kW.[4]

Scharnhorst and *Gneisenau* were also fitted with FuMO 22, FuMO 27 and FuMO 26 radar sets. With the outbreak of war, radar development became extremely complex, with the needs of the three fighting services resulting in separate developments to meet their individual and respective requirements. In each case a different system of code designation was adopted. It was only in 1943 that a standardised system of designation for radar sets was introduced across the three armed services. Prior, there existed no fewer than six different classifications.

Early sets were simply referred to as DeTe I, DeTe II and so forth, DeTe being and abbreviation of *Dezimeter-Teligraphie* [Decimeter radio], the first German codeword for radar. When the family of radar sets produced in Germany began to grow, this system was found to be insufficient, whereupon Arabic numbers were introduced, with 100–199 being reserved for naval tactical sets which worked on a wavelength of 80cm. In 1938 a more specific designation system had been introduced which gave fuller details of the set. For example, the first set which was installed aboard the pocket battleship *Admiral Graf Spee* was the FMG 39G (gO). In this, 'FMG' stood for *Funkmessgerät* [radar device]; '39' referred to the year of introduction (1939); 'G' stood for GEMA, the manufacturer of the set; 'g' was the frequency code (335–430MHz); while 'O' referred to the type of aerial installation, in this instance, a radar tower on top of the rangefinder tower.

In 1943 the designations were replaced by a standardised system which gave code letters for the type of set and a running number. Existing radar sets were subsequently

Photographed whilst an Arado seaplane was being hoisted aboard, the radar sets atop the director tower and on the rear superstructure can be clearly seen. (*Author's Collection*)

reclassified under this system with the FMG 39G (gO) becoming the FuMO 23. Codewords for the sets were also retained. As such Freya radar sets continued to be referred to as such by their operators. FuMO stood for *Funkmess-Ortung* [radar-direction finder, active ranging].

In November 1939 both *Scharnhorst* and *Gneisenau* were equipped with an 81.5cm (368MHz) FuMO 22 radar set, which was situated in a tower located above the forward rangefinder tower. The 6.5x19.6ft (2x6m) mattress antenna on the front of the tower rotated with the 34.4ft (10.5m) rangefinders, so that the result of both instruments could be compared. The structure was crowned by an open battle-observer's post. *Scharnhorst* and *Gneisenau* were the only capital ships of the Kriegsmarine to have this 'open' type of battle-observer post.

During the summer of 1941, whilst in Brest, both ships were fitted with a FuMO 27 radar on the aft rangefinder tower. The FuMO 27 had a range of approximately 18.6mi (29.99km) and also featured a mattress antenna which measured 6.5x13.1ft (2x4m). A FuMO 27 set was later installed on the forward director tower whilst at Brest.

Prior to conducting Operation Cerberus, more commonly known as the Channel Dash, *Scharnhorst* was equipped with a FuMB7 Timor passive antenna on the rear of the foretop, opposite the FuMO 27. The Timor measured 6.5x13.1ft. Once back in Germany, the passive radar sets aboard *Scharnhorst* were significantly revised. The Timor set was relocated to the front of the foretop rangefinder below the FuMO 27

A FuMB Ant. 4 Sumatra radar photographed on the heavy cruiser *Prinz Eugen*. Aboard the *Scharnhorst*, Sumatra radar was installed on all four handrails around the foretop gallery and on the tripod railings of the aft mast. (*NH 96455, US Naval History and Heritage Command*)

antenna, while the antenna of the FuMO 27 were moved higher up. FuMB Ant. 4 Sumatra radar search receiver antennas were installed on all four hand rails around the foretop gallery and on the tripod railings of the aft mast. On the mast heads, FuMB 3 Bali passive radar search receivers were installed along with a Palau antenna, which was mounted on top of the aft rangefinder.

In 1943, following the operation to bombard Allied installations on the island of Spitzbergen, the FuMO 27 sets aboard *Scharnhorst* were both replaced by FuMO 26 sets. In the foretop position, a 9.84x21.32ft (3x6.5m) horizontally polarised, common mode antenna was installed. At the same time the Timor set was removed. Aft, the FuMO 26 was provided with a 6.5x21.32 (2x6.5m) antenna with vertical polarisation.

The main battery turrets of the Scharnhorst-class were equipped with stereoscopic optical rangefinders, which were used to measure the distance to the target. The rangefinders used a pair of binoculars to triangulate the position of a target and determine its range. The stereoscopic principle allowed for the precise measurement of distances by comparing two slightly offset images of the target. The rangefinder was integrated into the roof of the turret. The turrets also featured a 34.4ft (10.5m) rangefinder. In the case of turret 'Anton', the 34.4ft rangefinder was removed from both *Scharnhorst* and *Gneisenau* in 1941.

FuMB Ant. 3 Bali radar receiver antennas photographed aboard the *Prinz Eugen*. Aboard *Scharnhorst* the Bali antennas were installed atop the mast heads. (*NH 96453, US Naval History and Heritage Command*)

The forward turrets of *Gneisenau* photographed during gunnery trials off Rügen in the Baltic, 1938.

The rangefinder hood on the starboard side of turret 'Caesar' aboard either *Scharnhorst* or *Gneisenau*. (*NH 102531, US Naval History and Heritage Command Center*)

The ships of the Scharnhorst-class were also equipped with four *Stabilisierter Leitstand* [stabilized director post] fire control systems which were utilised by the heavy anti-aircraft armament. All capital ships of the Kriegsmarine were equipped with the *Stabilisierter Leitstand*, though it may be noted that the number installed aboard the capital ships of the Kriegsmarine varied between one and four. The system measured distance, bearing and height of the target. Angles for bearing and height

Hitler standing in his motorcade in front of the *Scharnhorst*, 1 April 1939, whilst at Wilhelmshaven for the launch of the *Tirpitz*. The spherical *Stabilisierter Leitstand* 6 anti-aircraft directors can be clearly seen on the forward superstructure and funnel. (*Chris Thornton*)

were taken through an optical sight while the distance to the target was measured with a stereoscopic rangefinder.

The director post of the *Stabilisierter Leitstand* was stabilised on three axes against pitch and roll, so that measurements were taken in a horizontal plane. The director post was also stabilised against yaw which served to keep the director post trained on the target even when the ship was executing a turn. The measured data was processed by an analogue computer [*Rechengerät*] which calculated the settings for the anti-aircraft guns.

In operation, the artillery officer responsible for the anti-aircraft guns, typically the second artillery officer, assigned targets to the *Stabilisierter Leitstand*. From the anti-aircraft operation post, targets were selected with the *Zielanweisegerät* [target selection devices] (ZAG) which transmitted the bearings of the target to the *Stabilisierter Leitstand*. The *Zielanweisegerät* was also stabilised on three axes. A switchboard in the anti-aircraft operation post was used to configure which anti-aircraft battery or batteries a *Stabilisierter Leitstand* was guiding.[5]

The *Stabilisierter Leitstand* was manned by four people: two aimers, who measured the bearing and height of the target, the ranger finder and the control

Inside the cylinder of the *Stabilisierter Leitstand* showing the access to the director post located on top of the cylinder. This photograph was taken onboard the *Bismarck*. (*Bundesarchiv Bild* 193-06-2-07)

The superstructure and SL-6 directors of the *Scharnhorst*. (*Chris Thornton*)

officer. The two aimers sat with their backs to the target, while the control officer and range finder sat facing the target. Once a lock on the target had been acquired, the control officer signalled permission to fire to the director computer.[6] From that point measurement data could be fed into the director computer either intermittently or in a continuous modus. Due to the range of aircraft targets changing quickly, the continuous mode was generally used to feed the measurement data into the computer.[7]

Each *Stabilisierter Leitstand* had its own anti-aircraft director computer. The angles and range measured by the *Stabilisierter Leitstand* were transmitted to the director computer, which also calculated the fuse settings and triggered the firing clock. The fuse-setting mechanism was mounted on the outside of the anti-aircraft battery's protective shield. The computer would issue a horn signal when the round was set and had to be loaded into the gun, before giving a bell signal when the gun had to be fired.

The two ships of the Scharnhorst-class were equipped with four *Stabilisierter Leitstand* (SL) 6s for directing the heavy anti-aircraft armament. The SL-6 which equipped the Scharnhorst-class weighed 46t.[8] Two of the SL-6s were fitted on the port and starboard sides of the forward superstructure while the second pair was mounted on the port and starboard sides of the funnel.

Members of the crew of the *Scharnhorst* board the ship prior to the commissioning ceremony. In the background, the portside SL-6 anti-aircraft director abreast the funnel can be seen. (*Author's Collection*)

8

Boats

The ships of the Scharnhorst-class were equipped with a large number of various types of boat, which were utilised for a variety of purposes. The boats carried aboard the ships of the Scharnhorst-class included:

1. One admiral's barge [*Admiralsboot*]: for use by the squadron commander and his staff. They were stowed on the inner cradles on the starboard side of the funnel.
2. Three transportation boats [*Verkehrsboote*]: used for moving men and stores between ships and the shore. They were stowed on the outer cradles on both sides of the funnel and on a cradle in front of the funnel.
3. One motor pinnacle [*Motorpinasse*]: stowed on the inner cradles on the port side of the funnel
4. Two motor yawl [*Motorjollen*]: stowed on cradles on the upper deck below the aircraft hangar. They were removed from the ships in mid-1939.
5. Two yawl 1st class [*Jollenklass I*]: powered by oar, and stowed inside the row cutters on both sides of the aircraft hangar. They were removed from *Scharnhorst* and *Gneisenau* in late 1940.
6. Four row cutters 2nd class [*Kutterklasse II*]: used for sport and recreational purposes, as well as emergencies. Two of the cutters were stowed in a ready-use position in davits on the upper deck in front of the forward pair of SK C/28 L/55 guns. The remaining two cutters were stowed on cradles on both sides of the aircraft hangar. Two of the cutters and the davits on the upper deck would be removed in late 1940.[1]
7. The boats were supplemented by dinghies, which were stowed in cradles on both sides of the aircraft hanger, as well as by life rafts and inflatable boats, which were kept in storage boxes and stowed in various locations on the superstructure.

Type	Length	Weight
Admiral's barge	37.79ft (11.52m)	18,269.71lb (8,287kg)
Transportation boat	37.79ft (11.52m)	16,755lb (7,600kg)
Motor pinnacle	30.18ft (9.2m)	12,345.89lb (5,600kg)
Motor yawl	25.26ft (7.7m)	7,749.2lb (3,515kg)
Row yawl	19.6ft (6m)	2,209lb (1,002kg)
Row cutter	27.8ft (8.5m)	4,352lb (1,974kg)

Taken on the boat deck of the *Scharnhorst* between the forward superstructure and funnel, one of the ship's boats can be seen in the foreground. The ships of the Scharnhorst-class carried a variety of boats and launches.

9

Aircraft

Both vessels of the Scharnhorst-class were provided with aircraft facilities for the launching and recovery of aircraft. When completed, the ships of the class were equipped with two catapults. One catapult was located atop the hanger, which was located amidships behind the ship's funnel, while the second catapult was installed atop turret 'Caesar'. The catapult fitted atop turret 'Caesar' was later removed, leaving just one catapult.

Each of the ships was capable of carrying three aircraft. Upon commissioning, *Scharnhorst* carried Heinkel He-114 aircraft, while *Gneisenau* carried both Heinkel He-114s and Arado Ar-95s. Subsequently, on both ships, these aircraft were replaced by the Arado Ar-196. The intended role of the aircraft was reconnaissance, gunfire spotting, and if necessary, to serve as a form of local air cover for the ships.

While launched from a catapult, from ships like the *Scharnhorst* and *Gneisenau*, the aircraft had to land on the water and taxi alongside the ship before being hoisted aboard by one of the ship's cranes. On the port and starboard side of the ships situated amidships were cranes used to lift the aircraft through the roof of the hanger and place them on the catapult amidships, or on to the portside deck ship if the aircraft was to be launched from the catapult atop turret 'Caesar'. From the portside deck the aircraft would be picked up by a moveable crane, which could be collapsed on deck when not in use, and deposited on the aft catapult.[1] However, it was not possible to transfer the aircraft from crane to crane. This arrangement of placing the aircraft on deck to be picked up by the collapsible crane did not prove particularly efficient, and the collapsible crane and the catapult atop turret 'Caesar' were removed before the outbreak of war.[2] The amidships cranes were used to hoist the aircraft back on board the ships following landing.

In the armed forces of Germany at the time, all air activities were the responsibility of the Luftwaffe. This included the development, procurement, maintenance and operation of all ship-borne aircraft. Unlike in the Royal Navy, US Navy or Imperial Japanese Navy, there was never a separate German naval air arm. Indeed, even the aircraft which would have operated from the aircraft carrier *Graf Zeppelin*, had work not been suspended at the outbreak of war and she had been completed, would have been manned and controlled by the Luftwaffe.

The ships of the Scharnhorst-class were fitted with two catapults; amidships atop the hanger while the second was located atop turret 'Caesar' The catapult atop turret 'Caesar' was later removed. This photograph shows a close up of the catapult atop turret 'Caesar' aboard the *Scharnhorst*. (*NH 102536, US Naval History and Heritage Command Center*)

Member of the ship's crew aboard either *Scharnhorst* or *Gneisenau* cleaning the guns of turret 'Caesar' during the summer of 1939. The catapult atop the turret can be clearly seen. (*Author's Collection*)

Scharnhorst alongside at Wilhelmshaven, March 1940. While engineering ratings receive a lecture on machinery, atop turret 'Caesar', with the assistance of a floating crane, the catapult is removed from the turret. (*Simon Matthews*)

Crewmen painting the port crane aboard the *Scharnhorst*. The cranes were used to lift the aircraft through the roof of the hanger and to pace them on the catapult amidships or onto the portside deck if the aircraft was to be launched from the catapult atop turret 'Caesar'. The cranes were also used to lower and hoist some of the boats carried aboard the ships.

Heinkel He-114

The Heinkel He-114 was designed and constructed as a replacement for the Heinkel He-60. Making its maiden flight in 1936, the type was introduced into service in 1939. The fuselage of the He-114 and the floatation gear of the aircraft were conventional; however, its wing arrangement was highly unusual. The upper set of wings was attached to the fuselage by a set of cabane struts, as in a parasol monoplane, while the lower wings were of a much lesser span whilst having the same chord. Such aircraft are known as sesquiplanes, essentially biplanes with smaller lower wings.

Heinkel He-114 specification	
Crew	2 (pilot and observer)
Length	38ft, 2.5in. (11.65m)
Wingspan	44ft, 7.5in. (13.6m)
Height	17ft, 2in. (5.23m)
Engine	1xBMW 132K 9-cylinder radial engine 960hp
Speed	208mph (335km/h)
Maximum Service Ceiling	16,075ft (4,900m)
Range	571mi (920km)
Empty Weight	5,070lb (2,300kg)
Armament	1x7.92mm (0.312in.) MG 15 machine gun 2x110lb (50kg) bombs

A Heinkel He-114 A2 in flight. (*San Diego Air & Space Museum*)

A Heinkel He-114 seaplane on the catapult of the *Gneisenau*. (*NH 83614, US Naval History and Heritage Command Center*)

A Heinkel He-114 on the catapult of *Gneisenau*, 1939. (*Bundesarchiv DVM 10 Bild-23-63-02*)

The Heinkel He-114 was not a great success and was not built in large numbers. Indeed only 120 aircraft in all variants were constructed. The He-60 handled very well on the water but had been sluggish in the air. The He-114, meanwhile, had poor handling on the water and in the air was scarcely better than the He-60.[3] At the same time, the Arado Ar-196 was undergoing development, but it would require time before the type could be put into production. As a temporary solution the Luftwaffe decided not to retire the He-60 from service. Heinkel was informed that while the He-60 would remain in service temporarily, the He-114 would not be accepted into service. Instead, it would be offered for export. Though not accepted into service by the Luftwaffe, examples of the He-114, due to a lack of sufficient seaplanes, were used to fill the gap and met the immediate needs of the Kriegsmarine.

With a maximum speed of 208mph (335km/h) the Heinkel He-114 had a maximum range of 571mi (920km) and was manned by a crew of two: a pilot and an observer. The He-114 was armed with one 7.92mm (0.312in.) MG 15 machine gun in a flexible mount beside the observer and could carry two 110lb (50kg) bombs, one loaded under each wing.[4]

Arado Ar-95

The Arado Ar-95 was designed in 1935 to meet the requirement from the *Reichsluftfahrtministerium* [Reich Air Ministry] for a replacement for the Heinkel He-60 to fulfil the role of coastal patrol, reconnaissance and light attack aircraft.

Arado Ar-95 specifications	
Crew	2 (pilot and observer)
Length	36ft, 5in. (11.10m)
Wingspan	41ft (12.5m)
Height	11ft, 10in. (3.6m)
Engine	1xBMW 132De air-cooled 9-cylinder radial engine 880hp
Speed	193mph (310km/h)
Maximum Service Ceiling	24,000ft (7,300m)
Range	684mi (1,100km)
Empty Weight	2,450lb (1,111kg)
Armament	1xfixed forward-firing 7.92mm (0.312in.) MG 17 machine gun 1xflexible mount 7.92mm (0.312in.) MG 15 machine gun in rear cockpit 1x1,764lb (800kg) torpedo or 1,102lb (500kg) bomb

An Arado Ar-95 in flight. (*US Air Force*)

Taken in 1938, this photograph shows *Gneisenau* carrying both an He-114 and Ar-95. The He 114 is on the amidships catapult while the Ar-95 is on the catapult fitted atop turret 'Caesar'. (*NH 80977, US Naval History and Heritage Command Center*)

The prototype was powered by a BMW radial engine and made its maiden flight on 3 December 1936.[5] The first prototype was followed by a second prototype, which was powered by a Junkers Jumo 210 liquid-cooled engine.

The Ar-95 was a two-seat biplane seaplane. Designed by Arado's chief engineer, Walter Blume, the Ar-95 featured a monocoque construction of metal with wings of an all-metal construction and fabric undersides. The wings were foldable to enable ease of stowage. The tailplane of the Ar-95 along with the fin were composed of lightweight metals and employed a cantilever construction.[6]

The two prototypes were evaluated against the Focke-Wulf Fw-62 after which the BMW-powered prototype was considered worthy of further study, with an order for six aircraft being placed. The aircraft were subsequently sent to Spain for evaluation with the Condor Legion.

The Arado Ar-95 was not ordered by the German armed forces, although a handful of examples did see service aboard the *Gneisenau* in July 1938 as part of the evaluation of the aircraft. Instead, the Ar-95 was offered as an export as both a floatplane and a land-based aircraft. Six land-based variants of the aircraft were ordered by the Chilean air force and were delivered prior to the outbreak of war. An order for the Ar-95 was also placed by Turkey, which ordered the type in its floatplane configuration. The aircraft ordered by Turkey were taken over by Germany at the outbreak of war in 1939, whereupon they were used for training and reconnaissance in the Baltic.

Arado Ar-196

The Arado Ar-196 was designed to meet a requirement for an overwater reconnaissance aircraft which could operate from ships, shore bases along the coast, rivers and lakes. The Ar-196 was a low-wing monoplane powered by a nine-cylinder air-cooled BMW 132K radial engine which drove a three-blade variable-pitch propeller. This gave the aircraft a maximum speed of 194mph (312km/h).

Designed by Walter Blume, the Ar-196 made its maiden flight on 1 June 1937. The aircraft was a semi-cantilever low-wing aircraft.[7] The design of the fuselage was based on that of the Ar-95. The forward fuselage and wings were metal-skinned, with a fabric covering used for the rear fuselage and tail assembly.[8] The aircraft made extensive use of hydronalium, an alloy known for its resistance to corrosion in maritime environments. The two floats on which the aircraft rode were used as fuel tanks.[9]

The variant of the Ar-196 that was carried aboard both the *Scharnhorst* and *Gneisenau* was the A-3 variant which had a range of 665mi (1,070km) and a service ceiling of 23,000ft (7,020m). With regards to weaponry, the Ar-196 A-3 was equipped with two 20mm MG FF cannon, one of which was sited in each wing, a 7.92mm (0.312in.) MG 17 machine gun in the cowling and a 7.92mm MG 15 machine gun in the rear cockpit. In addition to this, beginning with the A-2 variant, the Ar-196 was equipped with a bomb rack under each wing, which enabled the aircraft to carry two 110lb (50kg) bombs.[10]

Arado Ar-196 A-3 specifications	
Crew	2 (pilot and observer)
Length	36ft (11m)
Wingspan	41ft (12.4m)
Height	14ft (4.4m)
Engine	1xBMW 132K 9-cylinder air-cooled radial piston engine 947hp
Speed	194mph (312km/h)
Maximum Service Ceiling	23,000ft (7,020km)
Range	665mi (1,070km)
Empty Weight	6,592lb (2,990kg)
Maximum Take-off Weight	8,200lb (3,720kg)
Armament	2x20mm MG FF cannon 1x7.92mm (0.312in.) MG 17 machine gun 1x7.92mm (0.312in.) MG 15 machine gun 2x110lb (50kg) bombs)

The raising of an Arado Ar-196 from the hangar aboard either *Scharnhorst* or *Gneisenau*. (*Author's Collection*)

Taken aboard *Scharnhorst* whilst in Brest, the wings of one of the ship's Ar-196 can be seen to have been extended prior to the aircraft being lifted onto the catapult. (*Author's Collection*)

An Arado Ar-196 on the amidships catapult of the *Gneisenau*, c. 1940. (*NH 83610, US Naval History and Heritage Command Center*)

An Ar-196 moments before being launched from the amidships catapult of the *Gneisenau*, c. 1940. (*NH 82411, US Naval History and Heritage Command Center*)

An Arado Ar-196 moments after being launched from the catapult of the *Gneisenau*, 1940. (*NH 71325, History and Heritage Command*)

10

Comparison Data

Ship	*Scharnhorst*	*Tirpitz*	HMS *King George V*	HMS *Rodney*
Class	Scharnhorst-class	Bismarck-class	King George V-class	Nelson-class
Length	771ft (234.9m)	823.6ft (251m)	745ft (227m)	710.2ft (216.5m)
Beam	98ft (30m)	118.1ft (36m)	103ft (31m)	106ft (32.3m)
Draught	32ft (9.8m)	30.6ft (9.3m)	32.6ft (9.9m)	31ft (9.4m)
Displacement (Full Load)	38,100t	52,600t	42,200t	38,030t
Speed (kt)	31	30	28	23
Main Armament	9x28cm (11in.) SK C/34	8x38cm (15in.) SK C/34	10xBL 14in. Mk VII Naval Gun	9xBL 16in. (406mm) Mk I Gun
Maximum Main Armament Range	25.4mi (40.9km)	22.69mi (36.51km)	20.73mi (33.36km)	22.6mi (36.37km)
Complement	1,669	2,065	1,314–1,631	1,314 (1,361 as flagship)
No. of Aircraft Carried	3	4	4	2

JSS *Washington*	*Littorio*	*Dunkerque*	*Richelieu*
Vorth Carolina-class	Littorio-class	Dunkerque-class	Richelieu-class
29ft (222m)	780.1ft (237.76m)	703.9ft (214.5m)	813ft (247.9m)
08ft (33m)	107.8ft (32.82m)	102ft (31.08m)	108ft (33m)
8ft (12m)	31ft (9.6m)	28.7ft (8.7m)	32ft (9.7m)
6,100t	45,236t	35,500t	47,548t
.8	31.4	29.5	30
×16in./45-calibre Aark 6 Gun	9×381mm (15in.) Cannone da 381/50 Ansaldo M1934	8×330mm (13in.) 50 Modèle 1931 Gun	8×380mm (15in.)/45 Modèle 1935
1mi (33.7km)	22mi (35km)	25.22mi (40.6km)	25.9mi (41.7km)
,880	1,830	1,381 to 1,431	1,620
	3	2	3

Endnotes

Introduction

1. E. Gröner, *German Warships 1815–1945 Vol. I: Major Surface Vessels* (Annapolis: Naval Institute Press, 1990), p. 31.
2. W. Churchill, *The Second World War: Volume V Closing the Ring* (London: Folio Society, 2003), p. 245; D. van der Vat, *The Atlantic Campaign* (New York: Harper and Row, 1988), p. 82; BR 1736 (48) (2) Naval Staff History of the Second World War, *Home Waters and the Atlantic Volume II, 9th April 1940–6th December 1941* (1961), pp. 14–15.
3. F. E. McMurtri (ed.), *Jane's Fighting Ships 1940* (London: Sampson Low, Marston & Co, 1940), pp. 212–13.
4. Gröner, *German Warships*, p. 32; Basil Collier, *The Defence of the United Kingdom: History of the Second World War* (London: Her Majesty's Stationary Office, 1957), p. 99.
5. Article 190, *Treaty of Versailles* (1919).
6. D. Knowles, *Tirpitz: The Life and Death of Germany's Last Great Battleship* (Stroud: Fonthill Media, 2018), p. 16.
7. Ibid., p. 18; A. Preston, *The World's Worst Warships* (London: Conway Maritime Press, 2002), p. 117.
8. W. H. Garzke, R. O. Dulin, *Battleships: Axis and Neutral Battleships in World War II* (Annapolis: Naval Institute Press, 1985), p. 128.
9. D. Knowles, *Scharnhorst and Gneisenau* (Stroud: Fonthill Media, 2023), pp. 19–20.
10. Garzke, Dulin, *Battleships*, p. 130.
11. S. Breyer, *Battleships and Battlecruisers, 1905–1970* (New York: Doubleday & Company, 1974), p. 294.
12. G. Williamson, *German Battleships 1939–45* (Oxford: Osprey Publishing Limited, 2003), p. 8.
13. Knowles, *Scharnhorst and Gneisenau*, pp. 65–71.
14. J. Rohwer, *Chronology of the War at Sea 1939–1945: The Naval History of World War Two* (Annapolis: Naval Institute Press, 2005), p. 26.
15. Knowles, *Scharnhorst and Gneisneau*, p. 96.

16. P. Bishop, *Target Tirpitz: X-Craft, Agents and Dambusters—The Epic Quest to Destroy Hitler's Mightiest Warship* (London: Harper Press, 2012), p. 49.
17. Garzke, Dulin, *Battleships*, pp. 149–50.
18. Williamson, *German Battleships 1939–45*, p. 18.
19. S. Breyer, *The German Battleship Gneisenau* (West Chester: Schiffer Publishing, 1990), p. 34.
20. Garzke, Dulin, *Battleships*, p. 153.
21. Ibid., p. 161.
22. Gröner, *German Warships*, p. 32; Garzke, Dulin, *Battleships*, p. 153.
23. Breyer, *The German Battleship Gneisenau*, p. 34.
24. R. Garrett, *Scharnhorst and Gneisenau: The Elusive Sisters* (London: Hippocrene Books, 1978), p. 121.
25. Knowles, *Tirpitz*, p. 99.

1. General Characteristics

1. Knowles, *Scharnhorst and Gneisenau*, p. 23.
2. Ibid., p. 23, p. 48.
3. Ibid., p. 59.
4. Ibid., p. 23.
5. Gröner, *German Warships*, p. 31.

2. Armament

1. Gröner, *German Warships*, p. 99.
2. J. Campbell, *Naval Weapons of World War Two* (Annapolis: Naval Institute Press, 2002), p. 219.
3. Ibid.
4. Breyer, *Battleships and Battlecruisers*, p. 294
5. Garzke, Dulin, *Battleships*, p. 130.
6. Knowles, *Scharnhorst and Gneisenau*, p. 19.
7. Breyer, *Battleships and Battlecruisers*, p. 294; Knowles, *Scharnhorst and Gneisenau*, p. 21.
8. Knowles, *Scharnhorst and Gneisenau*, p. 21.
9. Campbell, *Naval Weapons of World War II*, p. 231.
10. S. Draminski, *The Battleship Scharnhorst* (Oxford: Osprey Publishing, 2021), p. 17.
11. Ibid.
12. Ibid.
13. Knowles, *Scharnhorst and Gneisenau*, p. 25
14. Draminski, *The Battleship Scharnhorst*, pp. 17–18.
15. Campbell, *Naval Weapons of World War II*, p. 241.
16. Draminski, *The Battleship Scharnhorst*, p. 18.
17. Campbell, *Naval Weapons of World War II*, p. 241.
18. Knowles, *Scharnhorst and Gneisenau*, p. 28.

19. Knowles, *Tirpitz*, p. 32.
20. Campbell, *Naval Weapons of World War II*, p. 241.
21. Draminski, *The Battleship Scharnhorst*, p. 20.
22. Knowles, *Scharnhorst and Gneisenau*, p. 28
23. Campbell, *Naval Weapons of World War II*, p. 247.
24. Knowles, *Scharnhorst and Gneisenau*, p. 28
25. Draminski, *The Battleship Scharnhorst*, p. 22.
26. Ibid.
27. Campbell, *Naval Weapons of World War II*, p. 256.
28. Draminski, *The Battleship Scharnhorst*, p. 22.
29. Campbell, *Naval Weapons of World War II*, p. 258.
30. Draminski, *The Battleship Scharnhorst*, p. 23.
31. Campbell, *Naval Weapons of World War II*, p. 263.
32. Knowles, *Scharnhorst and Gneisenau*, p. 28
33. Campbell, *Naval Weapons of World War II*, p. 263.

3. Hull Structure

1. Knowles, *Scharnhorst and Gneisenau*, p. 30.
2. Draminski, *The Battleship Scharnhorst*, p. 9.
3. Ibid.
4. Ibid., p. 10.
5. Ibid., p. 59.
6. Gröner, *German Warships*, p. 31.
7. Ibid., p. 11.

4. Armour

1. Draminski, *The Battleship Scharnhorst*, p. 12.
2. Ibid; Gröner, *German Warships*, p. x; Knowles, *Scharnhorst and Gneisenau*, p. 30.
3. Draminski, *The Battleship Scharnhorst*, p. 12; Knowles, *Scharnhorst and Gneisenau*, p. 31.
4. Knowles, *Scharnhorst and Gneisenau*, p. 30.
5. Gröner, *German Warships*, p. 31.
6. Garzke, Dulin, *Battleships*, p. 182.
7. Draminski, *The Battleship Scharnhorst*, p. 12.
8. Garzke, Dulin, *Battleships*, p. 183.
9. Knowles, *Scharnhorst and Gneisenau*, pp. 30–31.
10. Draminski, *The Battleship Scharnhorst*, p. 13.
11. Knowles, *Scharnhorst and Gneisenau*, p. 31.
12. Draminski, *The Battleship Scharnhorst*, p. 14.
13. Gröner, *German Warships*, p. 31.
14. Draminski, *The Battleship Scharnhorst*, p. 14.
15. Garzke, Dulin, *Battleships*, p. 185.

16. Draminski, *The Battleship Scharnhorst*, p. 15.
17. Garzke, Dulin, *Battleships*, p. 185.
18. Ibid., pp. 185–86.
19. Ibid., p. 186.

5. Propulsion

1. Knowles, *Scharnhorst and Gneisenau*, p. 33.
2. Breyer, *Battleships and Battlecruisers 1905–1970*, p. 295.
3. Knowles, *Scharnhorst and Gneisenau*, p. 33.
4. G. Koop, K.-P. Schmolke, *Battleships of the Scharnhorst Class: The Scharnhorst and Gneisenau, The Backbone of the German Surface Forces at the Outbreak of War* (London: Greenhill Books, 1999), p. 25.
5. Draminski, *The Battleship Scharnhorst*, p. 15.
6. Ibid.
7. Koop, Schmolke, *Battleships of the Scharnhorst Class*, p. 28.
8. Ibid.
9. Ibid.
10. Ibid., p. 24.
11. Gröner, *German Warships*, p. 31.
12. Knowles, *Scharnhorst and Gneisenau*, p. 34.
13. Ibid., p. 223.

6. Electrical Power

1. Gröner, *German Warships*, p. 11.
2. Draminski, *The Battleship Scharnhorst*, p. 15.
3. Ibid., p. 16.

7. Radar and Rangefinders

1. Knowles, *Scharnhorst and Gneisenau*, p. 32.
2. H. von Kroge, *GEMA: Birthplace of German Radar and Sonar* (Bristol: Institute of Physics Publishing, 2000), p. 20; F. A. Kingsley (ed.), *The Applications of Radar and Other Electronic Systems in the Royal Navy in World War 2* (Basingstoke: Macmillan Press, 1995), p. 271.
3. G. Galati, *100 Years of Radar* (New York: Springer International, 2016), p. 70.
4. Garzke, Dulin, *Battleships*, pp. 188–89.
5. S. Draminski, *The Battleship Bismarck: Anatomy of the Ship* (Oxford: Osprey Publishing, 2018), p. 24; P. Schmalenbach, *Die Geschichte der deutschen Schiffsartillerie* (Herford: Koehler, 1993), p. 121.
6. Schmalenbach, *Die Geschichte der deutschen Schiffsartillerie*, p. 123.
7. Ibid., p. 126.
8. G. Koop, K.-P. Schmolke, *The Heavy Cruisers of the Admiral Hipper Class* (London: Greenhill Books, 2001), p. 201.

8. Boats

1. Draminski, *The Battleship Scharnhorst*, p. 28.

9. Aircraft

1. P. Schmalenbach, *German Battlecruisers Scharnhorst and Gneisenau: Profile Warship 33* (Windsor: Profile Publications, 1973), p. 209.
2. Williamson, *German Battleships 1939–45*, p. 10.
3. Knowles, *Scharnhorst and Gneisenau*, p. 36.
4. D. Donald (ed.) *Warplanes of the Luftwaffe: A Complete Guide to the Combat Aircraft of Hitler's Luftwaffe from 1939 to 1945* (London: Aerospace, 1994), p. 107; J. R. Smith, A. Key, *German Aircraft of the Second World War* (London: Putnam & Company Ltd, 1972), p. 268.
5. P. de Jong, *Arado Ar 196 Units in Combat* (Oxford: Osprey Publishing, 2021), p. 8.
6. J. A. Kranzhoff, *Arado: History of an Aircraft Company* (Atglen: Schiffer Books, 1997), pp. 76–77.
7. Ibid., pp. 81–82.
8. Ibid.
9. De Jong, *Arado Ar 196*, p. 10.
10. Knowles, *Tirpitz*, pp. 42–43.

Bibliography

Article 190, *Treaty of Versailles* (1919)

Bennett, G. H., *Hitler's Ghost Ships: Graf Spee, Scharnhorst and Disguised German Raiders* (Plymouth: University of Plymouth Press, 2012)

Bishop, P., *Target Tirpitz: X-Craft, Agents and Dambusters—The Epic Quest to Destroy Hitler's Mightiest Warship* (London: Harper Press, 2012)

BR 1736 (48) (2) Naval Staff History of the Second World War, *Home Waters and the Atlantic Volume II, 9th April 1940–6th December 1941* (1961)

Breyer, S., *Battleships and Battlecruisers, 1905–1970* (New York: Doubleday & Company, 1974)

Breyer, S., *The German Battleship Gneisenau* (West Chester: Schiffer Publishing, 1990)

Busch, F.-O., *The Drama of the Scharnhorst* (Ware: Wordsworth, 2001)

Campbell, J., *Naval Weapons of World War Two* (Annapolis: Naval Institute Press, 2002)

Churchill, W. S., *The Second World War: Volume V Closing the Ring* (London: Folio Society, 2003)

Collier, B., *The Defence of the United Kingdom: History of the Second World War* (London: Her Majesty's Stationary Office, 1957)

De Jong, P., *Arado Ar 196 Units in Combat* (Oxford: Osprey Publishing, 2021)

Donald, D., *Warplanes of the Luftwaffe: A Complete Guide to the Combat Aircraft of Hitler's Luftwaffe from 1939 to 1945* (London: Aerospace, 1994)

Draminski, S., *The Battleship Bismarck: Anatomy of the Ship* (Oxford: Osprey Publishing, 2018)

Draminski, S., *The Battleship Scharnhorst* (Oxford: Osprey Publishing, 2021)

Ford, K., *Run the Gauntlet: The Channel Dash 1942* (Oxford: Osprey Publishing 2012)

Galati, G., *100 Years of Radar* (New York: Springer International, 2016)

Gardiner, R., *Conway's All The World's Fighting Ships 1922–1946* (Annapolis; Naval Institute Press, 1980)

Garrett, R., *Scharnhorst and Gneisenau: The Elusive Sisters* (London: Hippocrene Books, 1978)

Garzke, W. H., Dulin, R. O., *Battleships: Axis and Neutral Battleships in World War II* (Annapolis: Naval Institute Press, 1985)

Gröner, E., *German Warships 1815–1945 Vol. I: Major Surface Vessels* (Annapolis: Naval Institute Press, 1990)
Grove, E., *German Capital Ships and Raiders of World War II: From Scharnhorst to Tirpitz, 1942–1944* (London: Routledge, 2002)
Harding, D., *Sink the Scharnhorst* (York: Benchmark Publishing, 2016)
Humble, R., *Hitler's High Seas Fleet* (New York: Ballantyne Books, 1971)
Jacobsen, A. R., *Scharnhorst* (Stroud: Sutton Publishing, 2003)
Johnston, I., McAuley, R., *The Battleships* (London: Channel 4 Books, 2000)
Kemp, P., *Escape of the Scharnhorst and Gneisenau* (London: Ian Allen, 1975)
Kingsley, F. A. (ed.), *The Applications of Radar and Other Electronic Systems in the Royal Navy in World War 2* (Basingstoke: Macmillan Press, 1995)
Knowles, D., *Scharnhorst and Gneisenau* (Stroud: Fonthill Media, 2023)
Knowles, D., *Tirpitz: The Life and Death of Germany's Last Great Battleship* (Stroud: Fonthill Media, 2018)
Konstam, A., *The Battle of North Cape: The Death Ride of the Scharnhorst 1943* (Barnsley: Pen and Sword, 2011)
Koop, G., Schmolke, K.-P., *Battleships of the Scharnhorst Class: The Scharnhorst and Gneisenau, The Backbone of the German Surface Forces at the Outbreak of War* (London: Greenhill Books, 1999)
Koop, G., Schmolke, K.-P., *The Heavy Cruisers of the Admiral Hipper Class* (London: Greenhill Books, 2001)
Kranzhoff, J. A., *Arado: History of an Aircraft Company* (Atglen: Schiffer Books, 1997)
Martiessen, A., *Hitler and His Admirals* (London: Secker, 1948)
McMurtri, F. E. (ed.), *Jane's Fighting Ships 1940* (London: Sampson Low, Marston & Co, 1940)
Potter, E. B., (ed.) *Sea Power: A Naval History* (Annapolis: Naval Institute Press, 1981)
Preston, A., *The World's Worst Warships* (London: Conway Maritime Press, 2002)
Ramsden, B., 'Sinking the *Scharnhorst*', *Blackwood's Magazine*, No. 1549 (1944)
Rohwer, J., *Chronology of the War at Sea 1939–1945: The Naval History of World War Two* (Annapolis: Naval Institute Press, 2005)
Schmalenbach, P., *Die Geschichte der deutschen Schiffsartillerie* (Herford: Koehler, 1993)
Schmalenbach, P., *German Battlecruisers Scharnhorst and Gneisenau: Profile Warship 33* (Windsor: Profile Publications, 1973)
Smith, R. J., Kay, A., *German Aircraft of the Second World War* (London: Putnam and Company Ltd, 1972)
Van Der Vat, D., *The Atlantic Campaign* (New York: Harper and Row, 1988)
Von Kroge, H., *GEMA: Birthplace of German Radar and Sonar* (Bristol: Institute of Physics Publishing, 2000)
Vulliez, A., Mordal, J., *Battleship Scharnhorst* (London: Hutchinson, 1958)
Williamson, G., *German Battleships 1939–45* (Oxford: Osprey Publishing, 2003)

Index